TEACHING ENGLISH
AS A
FOREIGN LANGUAGE

By the same author

TEACHING THE MOTHER TONGUE
  IN SECONDARY SCHOOLS
THE TEACHING OF WRITTEN ENGLISH
TEACHING ENGLISH GRAMMAR
EDUCATION AND THE TRAINING OF TEACHERS

TEACHING ENGLISH
AS A
FOREIGN LANGUAGE

P. GURREY

LONGMANS

LONGMANS, GREEN AND CO LTD
48 Grosvenor Street, London W.1

*Associated companies, branches and representatives
throughout the world*

First published 1955
Eighth impression by photolithography 1964

PRINTED IN GREAT BRITAIN
BY LOWE AND BRYDONE (PRINTERS) LTD., LONDON, N.W.10

CONTENTS

" He could write and read, not one book, not a dozen books, but any book that he lifted up, which was a wonder to them all. He could read even the books they had in their own languages, and the Bible translated by the English missionaries, and it was a wonder to hear their own tongues coming out of these black marks on white paper."

Too Late the Phalarope. Alan Paton.
(Cape, 1953)

PREFACE

THIS is a book for teachers of foreign languages. It discusses many of the problems that they have to face, and it describes methods that have been found effective for each stage of a learner's progress, and it explains the principles underlying them. It is concerned mainly with the teaching of English in schools in environments other than European, and gives prominence to the urgent needs for thorough learning of the language that is the medium of instruction in schools and colleges. But as the principles and many of the methods and techniques of teaching languages are applicable everywhere, teachers of foreign languages in American and European schools will, no doubt, find enough here for them to think about, and enough for them to compare or contrast with their own methods and principles.

Some of the methods and suggestions described here have been adapted or devised in accordance with the results of research in the Gold Coast. I wish to express my gratitude to my helpers there for their criticisms and generous assistance in that research: to Mr. J. H. Andrews, Mr. R. R. Okyne, Mr. C. O. Botchway, Mr. P. Strevens, Mrs. Isabel Hope and Professor C. E. Smith; I also welcome this opportunity of thanking all those teachers who have invited me into their classrooms to observe their work and to teach, especially those in Hungary, Finland, Norway and in the large number of schools in the Gold Coast that I visited or that sent in contributions for the research team to study.

I owe a special debt of gratitude to Professor C. B. Diltz of the Ontario College of Education for his help in correcting the proofs of this book.

Chapter 1

THE NEEDS OF THE TEACHER OF FOREIGN LANGUAGES

TEACHING a foreign language is hard work; but hard work will nearly always bring success, especially if a teacher persistently exerts himself to make his pupils do the work. Few people, however, realize what an unceasing expenditure of thought and energy is essential for teaching this subject. Of course some of the burden of teaching a foreign language can be carried by a textbook—" The English Reader," as it is usually called, or " The English Course "; but though the textbook provides much material and guidance—text, vocabulary, grammar and exercises—yet this material is language in print, and therefore is recorded language, not the language that is the purposeful expression of a living mind. The teacher therefore has to transform that silent, inactive array of printed symbols into living speech. He has to make all those words, phrases and sentences in the book play a useful part in some real situation, or imagined real situation. He must do this in order to ensure that the language that is being learned by his pupils is realistic and living. To achieve that, he will need to use all the skill he has, all his energies, and all his abilities of voice, mind, action, will; for he himself is the instrument, the language transformer of the cold printed word, giving out the sounds, tones, rhythms, which the new language uses to express meanings of all kinds—intellectual, emotional, purposeful.

We note, too, that the successful teacher especially needs vitality and enthusiasm to carry on the necessary oral work during the first years, when day after day, week after week, he must continually summon up fresh stores from ever-dwindling reserves, until by the end of the term, he can hardly avoid feeling drained and empty. Language teaching demands this expenditure of energy. It requires so much mental and physical activity, partly because so much oral work is essential, and partly because of the complexity of language learning. The teacher has to see that his pupils understand the language, that they learn how to pronounce it correctly, that they learn to read it and use it in speech and writing. To handle this complexity efficiently, a teacher needs to have a dozen different methods at his finger ends and a number of skills at his command.

All this is, of course, well known, but we should remind ourselves of the difficulties and demands of the task, for an understanding of them impels us to realize that the language teacher needs help. He needs help to view his task with a clear mind, to perceive how the complexities of language can be dealt with in a simple way, to see how different aspects of language teaching can be handled by ringing changes on the methods he has at his disposal, and he needs continual help to enable him to maintain his determination and enthusiasm.

The three things that a teacher needs for his language lessons are: a knowledge of the best and most effective methods to use, an understanding of the purpose and aim of each method he uses, and confidence and skill in his handling of them, with perseverance and courage to carry on the work with good humour and enjoyment.

The help which a teacher needs cannot, of course, be supplied merely by a book; because it is essential for the teacher himself to use his initiative and to exert his own energies, if those needs are to be satisfied. He must seek advice from others if he wishes to receive effective help; so he should discuss language-teaching problems with colleagues, visiting supervisors, training college lecturers; he should invite criticisms of his plans and of his actual teaching; and he should put his own methods of teaching languages, his procedures, teaching habits and mannerisms, his objectives and results, under the revealing microscope of his own critical and well-focused scrutiny. He should also study many books on language teaching. Some of these will certainly help him to see his problems more clearly; but above all he needs to renew and refresh his determination continually to improve in skill and efficiency. Then he will gradually acquire a greater mastery of the techniques and methods of language teaching, and with this a fresh interest in his work.

All that a book like this can hope to do is to set a teacher on the right road to see the principles more clearly, to select his aims more carefully, and to understand the purpose and procedure of his methods more completely and precisely. It is always helpful to review and re-consider the essentials of language teaching: the value of sound aims, the necessity for pupil activity, the importance of inspiring their interest, and of enabling them to enjoy the successful achievement of their tasks and ambitions.

It is no easy task, either to teach or to help a teacher to teach, a foreign language. But for the teacher, there is a special difficulty that is not commonly considered: it is the difficulty of overcoming the barrier of the pupils' mother tongue. For the mother tongue acts as a block in all the learners' language reactions, and impedes the learning of the new language because it is so firmly seated as the first language. Indeed, the mother tongue is so much a part of our mental lives and of our unreflecting consciousness, as well as of our automatic responses to experience, that usually we are not aware of language when we speak or listen or write. We are conscious then only of what we have in mind, what we want to say or to know; and so our minds concentrate on meanings, not on words as symbols. For language is a vessel carrying a load of meanings; and we do not perceive the words, in sound or written symbols, as words, but only as meanings. It is only when there is some ambiguity or misunderstanding or doubt that we become aware of the language symbols conveying meanings. But in using a new language we cannot at first avoid being aware of language symbols, and of attending to words, sentence-patterns and grammatical forms, instead of meanings. Thus, we see that using the mother tongue is a somewhat different linguistic process from first making use of a foreign language. This makes the task of the foreign-language teacher a task that requires special procedures and technical methods.

Furthermore, the mother tongue is so deeply embedded in our mental lives and inner consciousness that learning a second language requires at first a different reaction to language: one that is a re-orientation and in part a re-organization of consciousness. Therefore special exercises, certain kinds of language drill, and carefully devised methods are necessary to help the pupils to form new language habits. There also have to be very many repetitions at first in order to establish these new linguistic responses, and to ensure their re-occurrence when needed, and especially to increase the availability of all the elements of the new language, as these are learnt: words, structural patterns, inflections, tones, rhythms and pronunciations. Then, later, there is needed the constant use of the language in a variety of contexts and for a variety of purposes: in dialogue, stories, plays, questions, etc. This is necessary so that the new language may become a manageable medium of thought, communication and expression. So we see that the task is highly complicated, and that the training that a language teacher should have is by no means simple, or easy to carry out. In fact, the trainer of language teachers needs to have special gifts of mind and personality.

There is yet another aspect of this subject that does not often receive much consideration: how to make the foreign language learning contribute to the pupil's education. Indeed, we might ask, can it help to educate him ? Some people would no doubt reply: we are equipping him with a skill, so that he can educate himself. Or they might say: the task of equipping him with skill in using a language is so difficult and prolonged, that no time will be left to educate him. Some might even say that many pupils cannot learn a second language, and therefore the attempt cannot be educative. All these answers are wrong, even if they refer only to the pupils with the least ability. The learning of any new language can always help in the linguistic education and in the mental development of a pupil. For language is one of the main activities of mind, and mind is the main part of personality. If the new language, therefore, is taught in a way that is psychologically sound, it must contribute to the pupil's general growth, because it is sharpening his intellect and making it play over many kinds of knowledge and experience. But to promote this, the teacher has to use methods that foster intelligent thought, wider understanding and deeper sympathies, as well as linguistic skills. So the urgent and difficult question for the teacher is " What methods shall I use ? " Above all, the values of understanding and sympathy must always be kept in mind, in order that the foreign language teaching may bring something of permanent value to the pupil. There must be no acceptance of the short-sighted view that a mechanical language-skill is all that can be produced: for language, whether a vernacular or a foreign tongue, can touch life at its fullest and richest.

Chapter 2

GENERAL AIMS AND PARTICULAR OBJECTIVES

In teaching, it is highly desirable to know exactly what one is hoping to achieve, as it is in all great undertakings. If that can be clearly seen, then the best way of getting to work usually becomes evident. We ought therefore to consider carefully what we are trying to do when we are teaching a foreign language. As is well known, there are four general aims: to teach pupils to hear and understand the spoken language, to understand what they read, to speak the language and to write it. In short, to understand the spoken and written language, and to speak and write it. There are, then, four abilities to train: hearing, reading, speaking, writing—with understanding as the main ingredient in each. This indicates that our chief concern should not be about difficulties of pronunciation, growth of vocabulary, grammar and structure, but with language abilities. And it should always be the teacher's first concern to get the pupils' language abilities into action, for only when there is activity with language is there any language learning *at all*. This obvious fact should dominate the devising of method, the planning of work and the selecting of schemes for the language teaching in every class throughout the school.

In planning to develop the four language abilities, the aims of the teacher throughout a course will be to teach new words, and so build up a varied, well-balanced vocabulary; to teach new grammatical forms, usages, constructions, patterns; and to have all these elements of language used to express whatever the pupils have read or otherwise have in mind. He must also aim to teach his pupils to write passages of a page or so of clear, well-connected thought in correct language, with every point relevant to the topic they are writing about. Nevertheless, these aims are far too general to be of practical help to a teacher in the classroom. They are useful only for general guidance, and perhaps to suggest what should be achieved by the best pupils at the end of their school course.

So, in addition to his general plan with its general aims, a teacher should have a definite, clear-cut aim for each lesson. For if he tries hard to achieve a well-defined objective, even if he does not fully succeed, he will always give a lesson that is some help to his pupils—and we need not be so blind as to think that every lesson does that ! But if he has only a general objective, he will usually not help his pupils very much. An aim should usually be decided upon when beginning to prepare a lesson, so that it may help in the planning of the method. Having selected an objective for a lesson, or for a series of lessons, the teacher should strive his utmost to achieve it; for the striving will give just that extra pressure and urgent insistence that are nearly always needed to make the pupils' learning exact, and to fix the new elements of the language firmly in their minds and language habits.

It is also most rewarding to keep the distinction clear between a general aim and the particular objective for a lesson. For instance, instead of choosing a grammatical category, such as Tense,[1] for the objective of a grammar lesson, one Tense should be selected; for an early lesson the objective might be " to illustrate and use the Present

---

[1] To distinguish such words as ' object ' meaning thing or aim from Object, a part of a Predicate, and ' subject ', theme, topic, from Subject, the grammatical category, all grammatical terms are in capitals.

Continuous orally." It is essential to particularize and limit an objective. If he does this, a teacher will know exactly what he should do during the lesson. Here, for instance, he might begin by carrying out a number of obvious actions, saying each time what he is doing; he can then get his pupils to use that Tense, seeing that they do simple and natural actions, and that they say correctly what they are doing: " We are now speaking English "—" We are now sitting down "—" Now we are standing up "—" A car is passing the school "—" Two inspectors are visiting the school "—" Now the school bell is ringing."

A second lesson on the same Tense might be given. The general aim would be ' to teach some grammar '; even the limited aim ' to teach the Present Continuous ' is not precise enough. But the particular objective ' to illustrate the Present Continuous Tense and to have it well practised ' would be definite and detailed enough. This clear-cut definiteness of aim gives a lesson a focus which enables the teacher to see exactly what his pupils have to do in the lesson, and it helps the pupils to realize exactly what they have to master. It simplifies and focuses the preparation, and impels teacher and class to concentrate on the topic to be learnt.

A Reading Lesson might provide another illustration. " Just reading " is quite inadequate for an aim: is it to be reading aloud or silently ? Is it to develop one of the essential reading skills, or is it to provide material for a discussion or a composition ? If it is to be reading aloud, is the objective ' improvement in the oral expression of meaning ' ? Or is it to improve the pupils' enunciation, or their fluency of reading ? Is it to polish up pronunciation ? A teacher should choose a limited objective like one of these for a single lesson, rather than attempt two or more.

B

For success, a clear and definite objective is absolutely essential. If a teacher has a single, definite aim, then teacher and class can concentrate on one aspect of the whole subject and on one language activity, with the result that their efforts are not scattered and dispersed in all directions. Teacher and class are then going together in the same direction towards the same objective, and they are then all trying to reach some clearly seen goal, instead of going along blindly in an aimless journey without a known end (which happens sometimes, even in the best schools). The teacher should usually tell a class what the objective is: " Now you are going to use the Present Continuous Tense so many times that you will always use it correctly in the future," or " In this lesson you are going to practise rapid silent reading in order to learn how to get information quickly and accurately from books."

A teacher who thinks out clear aims finds other advantages: the preparation of his lessons is easier. It is easier because an aim usually helps him to select the material for a lesson, and to decide the kind of work his pupils should do on it, *e.g.* chorus repetitions, or oral question and answer, or written exercises, or reading aloud. If his aim is to improve grammatical correctness of written work, he will see at once that he must give sentence-completion exercises or oral drill. If his aim is to get more fluency and ease in his pupils' reading aloud, he will know that the class must first read the chosen passage silently, and then be questioned on it until they know it thoroughly before they read it aloud; for he knows that they will stumble or read badly if they do not fully understand the passage.

As we have said, a clear aim can help in the selection of material for a lesson; for instance, to teach rapid reading, easy stories are the best material; to teach exact comprehension, it is best to select informative passages, rather than stories or plays; to give practice in using a Tense, questions need to be framed which require answers containing that Tense; to explain the use of similar Tenses, such as the Present Perfect and the Simple Past, the narration of short incidents will be useful. Here is an example: " Yesterday when I *returned* home from shopping, I said to my brother: ' I *have forgotten* to post your letter.' He said: ' I am not surprised. Last week you *forgot* to buy some stamps for me.' To-day when I *arrived* home, I said: ' I *have* not *forgotten* to post your letters, and I *have* also *bought* some fish for your supper.' "

A young teacher may have some trouble at first in deciding exactly what objective to choose for a lesson, though he should always know clearly what his general aims are; and a well-experienced teacher may not have realized that he has had a definite objective for many of his lessons. But with careful thought, puzzling out precisely what he wants to achieve, and what are the immediate needs of his pupils, a teacher of languages can soon become expert in noting the objective that he should strive for; and once he is aware of the advantage, he very soon forms the habit of directing his efforts and those of his pupils on to a selected objective.

The technique of choosing a very limited objective for each lesson is a most fruitful aid to better teaching. It gives focus, and therefore concentration; it gives clarity and therefore better understanding; it gives precision and therefore more firmly established progress. The careful thinking out of detailed and well-defined objectives for lessons will do more than almost anything else to improve a teacher's work and to make it effective. Then with greater success and pleasure in his pupils' quicker progress, the teacher's interest and satisfaction in the work increase, and give him inspiration for further advances.

Chapter 3

BEGINNING TO SPEAK THE NEW LANGUAGE

THIS beginning period is all important, for " Well begun is half done." If therefore good pronunciation, absolutely correct grammar and sentence-structures are carefully taught, not a little later on but from the very beginning, there will be no need later to impose numerous corrective and remedial exercises. If absolutely correct language is insisted on from the beginning, then firm habits of correct language usage will be established, and there will be no need to disturb the foundations later by corrections and altera-tions. The subsequent gain will be considerable, for progress will continue smoothly from the first, and there will be no setbacks or halts. It is far far easier to teach new material than to eradicate old faults. And having to unlearn bad pronunciations and other incorrect usages is troublesome and retarding, even to the best pupils. And it is much more difficult to learn correct usages when incorrect forms and structures have been acquired, than to learn the correct usage at the start. Therefore it is vitally necessary for language learners to work at correct pronunciation, grammar and structure at the very beginning of learning a new language. It is fatal to defer insistence on correctness ' until the pupils are older,' for then the damage will have been done.

It would be excellent if beginners were taught only by the best teachers in the school, as is done in a few schools. Certainly these teachers would find it a much pleasanter task than they now suppose it to be, for young pupils beginning to learn a new language are always keen to work and are willing to carry out the numerous repetitions that are necessary for them. And they are always ready to strive intently for perfection, if their teacher insists on their trying to achieve it. But it is often not easy to arrange for the best teacher to take the beginners, though sometimes it might be possible for him to take the beginners and the top form, rather than the two top forms. Perhaps the best way out of the difficulty would be for some of the keener teachers who have a gift for teaching languages to specialize in this important work, and to receive recognition as specialists, with financial benefit attached. When such teachers had equipped themselves with a sound knowledge of phonetics and with the techniques for a finer handling of the Direct Method, they would be of great service in a school.

It is essential to have skilful teaching in this beginning period for four reasons. First, because children can learn correct pronunciation *only* from a teacher who has perfected his own pronunciation, and has mastered the art of teaching the sounds of a foreign language that differ from those of the mother tongue. Secondly, because it needs special skill, liveliness and energy to give a lot of young children in a large class enough practice in speaking a new language. Thirdly, because it needs unusual patience and persistence to keep on repeating correct sentences and correcting pronunciations, and to do this throughout a lesson with good humour. Fourthly, because it needs the skill of a gifted teacher to vary the ways of getting repetitions and corrections, and to turn these into enjoyable games in making strange sounds and in making up unexpected sentences. This skill is needed for making use of the very limited number of sentences and sentence patterns that the children have learnt, and for bringing in sufficient variations to secure attention and interest, and thus to lay a simple foundation of correct usage in the pupils' language habits.

The Importance of Correct Pronunciation at the very beginning. It is a sad thing to think that all over the world teachers are busily teaching *incorrect* pronunciations to thousands of children daily ! They do this because they do not understand the importance of correct pronunciation from the beginning; and they have not realized how much trouble one must take to learn to pronounce a foreign language correctly. Few of them know how difficult it will be for children to learn correct pronunciations when they have been taught the wrong ones first—and taught often with painstaking assiduity ! Why is this ? Is it not that teachers cannot teach correct pronunciations because their own teachers did not master the foreign sounds correctly, because no insistence on correctness was made at their training colleges or by their inspectors, education officers and headmasters ? To some extent this is true, but it is also because they themselves did not make up their minds to train their own ears to *hear* correctly, and to learn how the sounds were really made. The ultimate responsibility rests on the individual. Always, we may be sure, he could have found out what to do. So the simple question "Why teach incorrect pronunciations when you could teach correct ones ? " is unanswerable.

When there is so much well-informed opinion about language teaching, it seems strange that the extreme urgency for pupils' first pronunciations to be correct has not been widely recognized by teachers and those who are responsible for the training of teachers or for their efficiency in the classroom. The chief reason for this urgency is that a pronunciation once learned is more difficult to change than any other element of language. As we have said, the mother tongue speech habits are so strong that new habits in speaking can stand up to them, and establish themselves against their pressure, only after many repetitions, skilful teaching and continual effort.

Much careful thought has been given to the selection and teaching of a useful vocabulary of English; but pronunciation, with its complementary tone and rhythm, has been neglected, in spite of the warnings and advice of every phonetician of note. Moreover, many men and women who have been teaching for years have taken great pains to read widely in order to increase their vocabulary and improve their command of idiom; but very few have done all they could to improve their pronunciation of English. Usually, no doubt, they do not know that their pronunciation is not near enough to an accepted standard for perfect intelligibility; and many of them have not discovered how to improve their pronunciation, for it is not common knowledge. Yet it is within the power of nearly every teacher of English to achieve a level of speaking which is a very close approximation to the natural speech of a native speaker of English who speaks carefully and enunciates clearly. There is no merit or value in imitating the muffled or slovenly speech of a shy or careless Englishman (except for ' escape ' or secret service purposes).

The neglect of this subject has caused some important points to be overlooked in teaching, though they are obvious enough. The first is that nearly all language learners, children and adults, learn to pronounce a new language mainly by imitating the pronunciations of a teacher. In fact, this is the only way in which most learners can learn to speak a foreign language. Next we should note that even if the teacher's pronunciation is excellent (it very rarely is), pupils' ability to imitate pronunciation is often not good enough for them to profit from the model. It follows therefore that learners of foreign languages usually have to be taught how to imitate sounds; and great care has to be given to improving their ability to do this.

It was the phoneticians who discovered that the ear has to be trained to hear new sounds accurately, and that though most learners think they have heard the new sounds, yet actually they have heard only the sounds of their mother tongue that are near to the new foreign language sounds. We must, then, remember that most of our pupils are hearing only those sounds that their ears are accustomed to hear, and that their minds are accustomed to receive and respond to; and, more important still, that most of the sounds that are different from those of their mother tongue, they will not hear at all. Thus they make use of the sounds they habitually use—and their pronunciation is wrong from the start. Furthermore, even when a teacher speaks the foreign language with a faultless pronunciation, many of his pupils will not hear the correct sounds. This is an unfortunate fact, but it must be faced and countered. The remedy is easy to propose, though hard to carry out: the ears of the learners will have to be taught to listen. The learners will have to be taught to concentrate on hearing the new sounds, and their minds will have to be persuaded to attend to them. Then they will know what sounds to imitate; and if they do not then make them accurately, they must be taught how to use their speech organs, especially tongue and lips, so that their speech organs produce the correct sounds perfectly. And there is no reason at all why nearly all pupils should not make these sounds perfectly. But the teacher must have accurate knowledge of the practical phonetics of his own and of the new language. This cannot be stressed too strongly.

Speaking before Reading. The order, then, will be Listening before Reading or Speaking. But which should come first: reading or speaking ? It is indeed easier for those of us who read a great deal to learn to read a foreign language than to speak it; but children, and most adults too, should begin to learn to speak a new language before they try to read it. This is because the spoken language is the real language, and therefore is a more potent manifestation of it than the printed form, which is but a pale reflected shadow of a living activity of human beings. Therefore speaking must come after a short period of a week or two of listening to the new sounds. Reading should be delayed if possible for a year. To delay it for two years would be better; but this is not possible where pupils do not begin a second language until their fourth or fifth school year. In the Gold Coast two years of oral English is now the rule in most schools; and the wisdom of this is evident in the high standard of school children's spoken English throughout the country, especially in the Northern Territories. If only one year of speaking is possible before reading begins, an intensive course of listening and speaking would be necessary, with not less than eight lessons a week.

The Problem of thorough Practice in Speaking. To give a large number of young children adequate practice in speaking a new language requires some special skill in method, special liveliness of manner and voice, and a ready flow of well-controlled energy. For if the children are to learn to use the new language, they must have considerable practice in speaking it, even if their use of it will later be mainly reading. To give them this practice is possible with classes of twelve, or at most fourteen[1]; but when pupils are

---

[1] The size of many of the classes in the great Public Schools of England and Scotland (from ten to twenty) is one of the main reasons for the consistent success of those schools, and good evidence that the best education is possible usually only with small classes.

herded into classes of thirty-five or forty, or even forty-five and fifty, the task is heart-breaking. But what can a teacher who is worth his salt do ? He will need some " special skill in method," amongst other things, when he is faced with this exacting work.

Therefore the specialist teacher has to train himself to master the methods of producing successful oral work with large classes. He will know that his pupils must have plenty of practice in making up simple answers to copious and easy questions; so he will need something more than mere ability to use a method competently. With large classes success will depend on the way a method is carried out. That is why we have referred to " special liveliness of manner and voice." Very simple questioning, quick taking of answers, speed in passing from pupil to pupil, brief correcting of wrong answers, all these are necessary for good oral work with large classes. The teacher has to go at it with a keenly attentive mind, putting his energy into asking rapid questions, speeding up the answering, getting corrections by pupils made unhesitatingly, and reducing the pauses while a child thinks out a correct or full answer : there's no time to wait and think—not with a large class (to teach a large class to think needs another method).

Teacher and class have to be keyed up for this kind of language practice, eager and quick to question, to answer, to speak, to move, to correct, to write on the board or show meaning in mime. Keenness, activity, humour, liveliness of mind and manner: these are the qualities that are needed for good oral work; but above all, speed—otherwise few of the pupils will have sufficient practice. Minor mistakes can quickly be put right by having the correct sentence repeated, or by imitation of a fellow-pupil's correct sentence; but major grammatical mistakes must be left for another lesson: this is not the time for careful explanations. This is practice in speaking, not grammatical theorizing.

So every child should speak, and speak many times; therefore it is the teacher's task to push the speaking ahead, throwing out questions, getting several answers sometimes to one question before saying which are right, then picking on children who have not answered, or calling on a silent child to correct an easy mistake. He must drive the speaking along by every means possible to him, varying the technique whenever it begins to drag. Though he must always remember that, for good practice in speaking, sentences must be easy and the conversation on quite simple lines. Therefore new words and constructions will not be brought in, unless they are absolutely necessary. Speaking in order to practise the accurate use of new words and structures will need another kind of lesson altogether, a much slower and more careful one.

It must be emphasized here that in order to get numerous answers quickly and plenty of questions from a class, the ideas must be simple and the facts well-known, and they must be expressed only in the language that has been studied, understood and thoroughly practised previously. That is the secret of good oral practice: free and easy use of all the words, forms and sentences that have been well practised in expressing ideas that are familiar to the pupils and of everyday interest. Too often teachers think that they ought to enlarge vocabulary and introduce new grammar always and at any cost, not realizing that all pupils need time and practice to master what has been recently introduced to them. Enlargement of vocabulary and grammar are indeed important; but the plentiful use of what has been studied must at first have the chief place.

Corrections and Repetitions. There is here the third reason for highly skilled teaching of beginners: long-suffering patience and kindly persistence are needed, so that first incorrect efforts and attempts are gently but firmly replaced by correct pronunciation, use of words and grammar; and the correct sounds and forms and sentence patterns are practised over and over in order to develop correct language reactions and to establish correct speech. For just as a young bird, learning to fly, must use his wings, even if he falls, so the young pupil must speak the new language, even if his efforts are at first inept and incorrect. But like the parent bird, the teacher can foster those early falterings, and by quiet patience, clear speaking and encouragement, he can get the corrected speech repeated many times until it is said correctly. This naturally requires the sympathetic persistence of a far-seeing wisdom and intelligence. The teacher who knows that he must lay solid foundations will enjoy seeing that they are well and truly laid.

This early work calls for skilful invention, because an unvarying repetition of correct sentences, bluntly and doggedly insisted on, will produce only mechanical and, finally, inattentive responses. That kind of repetition will not encourage eager effort in trying to say sentences better and better each time; and it is most necessary to encourage these efforts. So instead of many repetitions of the same sentence that has been corrected, what is needed is a slight variation of a word or Tense or Number, each pupil making a slight change as the repetition goes round the class. The inflection or item that needed correction should not be changed, of course. But if each pupil has to introduce a variation in his sentence, however slight, that will help him to focus his mind on what he is saying, and will sustain the interest.

For instance, if a pupil has said: " I go school," on the pattern of his mother tongue, or of " I go home "; each pupil will have to make up a sentence like " I go to school," *e.g.* " We go to school," " The boys go to school," " He goes to school," and so on. If they have learnt the Possessives ' my,' ' your,' ' their,' then these, or any other items that fit in, should be used if the class has already practised them well. Then, when a number of sentences have been correctly produced, the teacher can propose another variation, *e.g.* one that introduces phrases expressing place: " I go to the market." The pupils then vary the new model sentence: " I go to the town," . . . to the store, . . . to the library, . . . to my father's farm, . . . to my uncle's shop.   The game, of course, is to have a sentence ready when the turn comes round, or better still, to have two ready, in case someone says your sentence before you.

The spirit of a game can be fostered by quick comment: " That's a good sentence "—" That's a new one "—" Good answer "—" I didn't know you knew that word." Or by asking at the end of a round such a question as: " Who didn't get caught out that time ? " By little devices and keen interest in individual progress, taking note of those who surmount the hurdle each time and of those who usually fall, a teacher can help everyone in the class to make an effort and to achieve the sharp focus of attention that is required for progress in language learning. For language abilities are brought into activity by attention and effort, and language learning results solely from activity of language abilities.

The above technique (each pupil thinking of a small variation for his sentence) is a simple example of teaching craftsmanship that many teachers, even excellent ones, often do not use, or use but rarely; and yet it saves time and trouble, and provides an easy and effective exercise. The procedure requires the class to be trained to carry out the exercise in a specified way, and without fresh instructions each time it is used. Here, for instance, a teacher might say: " Repeat this sentence round the class (or round half the class, or every other pupil—that makes a class think !), changing the first word." Or, if he has trained his class to vary sentences like this, he might simply say: " Ten sentences like this: ' The boys go to school.' " Then, having called on the first ten boys that were ready: " Now ten more, each to contain a new place to go to "; and then " Ten more with names of boys in the class going somewhere," and so on. The unexpected, though simple, demands for each new sentence, and the competition to get a sentence ready quickly enough, make up a game that the class will enjoy. Though the point of the game is not enjoyment, but to stimulate efforts to frame sentences quickly and correctly. It fosters lively activity, and for many pupils makes the effort of attention possible.

It has not been sufficiently emphasized in the training of language teachers that every class ought to be taught to carry out routine kinds of repetition and other simple exercises without the help of a teacher. All that is needed is for a class to be given an idea of what is required and exactly what the procedure is, the same procedure being used always for the same kind of exercise. The teacher then merely gives the signal, such as the name of the exercise, or a model sentence, and the class runs through it without hesitation. Every language teacher ought to drill his classes in this way, and to train them to run through many different kinds of exercises without his taking part, except to note mistakes. This kind of teaching technique gives some small responsibilities to the pupils, and in such a simple way that it can be introduced quite early. It saves the teacher's energies for lessons in which all his powers need to be fully in action.

It is undoubtedly true that language teachers, more than any others, should learn to conserve their strength and their output of nervous energy; because the drain on these in teaching the speaking of a new language is so heavy. It is a great gain if one is able to keep fresh and lively in order that most of the speech work can be a realistic, social experience, and not a dull book-thumbing or rule-thumping task.

Learning new Sentence Patterns. At first only a few sentence patterns can be learnt. Consequently a teacher will find it difficult to make the work interesting and natural. This again is another reason for teachers of beginners to acquire special skill. These sentence patterns (such as Subject plus Verb, or Subject plus Verb plus Object) have to be established in the pupils' speech habits before more complex or variant types of structure are encountered. Therefore it is essential at first for a teacher to have them used over and over again in order to fix them firmly in the conscious memory as well as in automatic speech habits. This must be done so that the normal word-order of the commonest sentence patterns become ingrained in the pupils' habits of thought. This is especially necessary for pupils whose mother tongue differs markedly in structure from English, or from whatever new language is being learned. For instance, pupils with German as their mother tongue will need much more practice in using subordinate clauses (unless they have first learned Latin) than will pupils speaking one of the Akan languages of the Gold Coast, Twi, Fante, Asante or one of their dialects, because these languages make use of the structure ' Subject—Verb—Object,' both in main and in subordinate clauses, as in English; though both English and the Akan languages have very many variations of this simple word-order.

The disadvantage of having to introduce new structures very gradually is that it restricts the number and nature of the ideas that can be expressed in the new language. This limitation makes it difficult to vary the subjects expressed and the content of sentences, and to give an air of reality to them. For instance, the sentence pattern " This is a . . ." can be used for only one purpose: to name or identify some thing; and " How tall (big, long, fat, etc.) is that . . . ? " is used only to ask questions about the qualities of things or people. We have to realize that every sentence pattern is a pattern of thought, not merely a verbal formula: it is a fixed organization of inter-related words and meanings which express a certain type of thought. Thus when we are thinking of an action ' that passes over on to some *thing*,' in some way affecting it, such as writing, eating, pushing, washing, making, we have a thought that includes thinking of some thing being affected by an action—a Transitive thought. But thinking of actions that do not affect some thing (other than the doer), we have an Intransitive thought which we express in an Intransitive sentence. Beginners therefore should not be encouraged to try to express in the new language whatever comes into their heads, for their ideas may require structures and forms of expression they have not learnt.

But a teacher specializing in teaching beginners can train himself to keep to the few sentence patterns that his pupils know, and also to make use of these in such a variety of situation that no unnatural monotony or mechanical response results. To take a simple example, the structure " Where is the . . . ? " need not be used in a dull way, by keeping rigidly to the questions in the book. By pretending that he has lost something, or cannot see something, a teacher can amuse a class by his acting, and can get fresh and amusing answers: this helps attention and stimulates the pupils to take an active part in the answering. Thus the teacher might pretend to search for his hat or his glasses, and the class will enjoy telling him " It is on your head, Sir."—" They are on your nose." There are limits to this play-acting; but other everyday incidents, involving the question " Where is . . . ? " can be devised. With young children the guessing game, when a coin or some other small article is hidden before the lesson, produces ample use of this structure, and of the pattern: " It is on the . . ."; and the use of these structures then has a purpose, and therefore reality.

The additional skill which every good teacher of young children tries to acquire is the devising of suitable and expressive actions to reveal the meaning and use of words taught. Mimed action, even if not very expert, gives life to a lesson, and ensures thorough learning, for what is seen is nearly always remembered; and meanings that are being revealed through action hold the attention of children and sharpen the focus. Actions suggest real life and arouse expectations of " What will happen next ? " Thus meanings and usages are far more firmly fixed in mind than if they were merely expressed verbally.

Chapter 4

THE DIRECT METHOD

THE success of the Direct Method in many parts of West Africa has indisputably proved that the teachers there understand the method properly and can handle it efficiently. They have shown that this method is not only a practical and useful example of good craftsmanship, but that it is easy to handle, and effective. It is to the credit of training colleges in Africa that this method is taught so well, and that there is such clear understanding among teachers of its value and procedures. Not all, however, use the method with a full realization of its exact purpose and application. Even some of those teachers who have proved that full confidence can be placed in it, and who are assured of its soundness and effectiveness, could get more out of it by applying it more fully, and by combining it with other methods.

The Direct Method can be used in conjunction with other methods because it is not properly a ' method ' at all. It is a principle, and it is one of the main principles of the psychology of language that can be directly translated into classroom procedure. It can, and should, be applied to almost all of the teaching of a foreign language: in the teaching of grammar, new words, new constructions, new sentence patterns. It is applied fully, though often without a teacher realizing it, in the *lecture expliquée*, in the singing of songs, telling stories, and in much dramatic work in the foreign language.

The Direct Method should not be thought of only as the close associating of words with the things named by them, though that certainly is the theory in its simplest terms. There is much more in it than that: the principle may be explained as the associating of word with thing, of thing with context, and of context with expression in the new language. Context may be idea, event, or whole situation; but the fullest application of the method is the associating of a complete thought expressed in words with the real experience that would give the occasion and impulse for the thought. For instance, the word ' watch ' is to be taught: the pupils look at one, and if possible touch it (touch brings such certainty to children). Then the teacher uses the word in a ' real ' experience, saying: " Look, I am winding my watch "; as he does so, the children all listen intently to the tiny clicks. So the *idea* of winding a watch is immediately associated with the words expressing the act. Of course the children know all about winding a watch; but their attention and interest in making sure that they will hear the clicks transform the small event into a fuller experience for them; and so the word ' watch ' becomes part of a larger unit of thought and understanding, reinforced by sense-perception, interest and enjoyment.

We note here, too, that the word has been associated with a complete context, an active one, not merely with a thing, referred to without interest or purpose. In addition the word ' winding ' is not first met with as a purely verbal form with a meaning that has to be memorized; but it has been encountered in a context of real life; they have seen the living person perform the action; they have heard the result of the action and the words that express action. The experience is real to them, and the language to be learned is an essential part of it, not just hooked on artificially: it has therefore played upon their minds with the purpose and significance of real language, even though it is so simple.

In addition, their interest, attention and pleasure have increased the completeness of their participation in a concrete, physical event, and thereby have strengthened their learning.

Learning a new language in this way, bit by bit, is more certain in result, richer in significance and more lasting than learning solely from ' the book.' A simple, physical action, like the one we have described, has been woven into a fuller, more continuous little event: teacher showing watch, pupils looking, touching, teacher winding, pupils hearing the clicks and *then* the sentence expressing the action. This kind of experience drives home the meaning of the new words and imprints them on mind and memory: if attention has been concentrated and interest fully alive, it will print them indelibly.

We have described this little event fully in order to show how very simple an experience in learning may be; there is no need to work out or describe elaborate incidents. But the degree of completeness will depend on the sophistication and maturity of the children. For instance, simple contexts, like the one above, will not always evoke enough interest and attention in a middle form to make the imprint of words on minds and memory firm enough for really successful learning; as a situation with a single sentence and simple action is too slight to make an impression on many classes.

What is needed is the full ' contextual situation ' of a living event. Using the same topic, we now must imagine a more significant story: the teacher pretending he is late and in a hurry to leave, keeps on looking at his watch. Then with an exclamation of annoyance, he holds it to his ear, then shakes it gently, and looks at it again: " Oh, dear ! It has stopped again. Did I wind it last night ? I always wind it at night; but did I last night ? " Thus he suggests

to the imaginations of his pupils some little everyday
' situation ' by his actions and words.

The virtue of the technique of building up a fairly full
situation is that attention is focused on simple dramatic
actions, and on the words and sentences that receive their
meanings from them. The children enter imaginatively into
the incident as if it were reality, and so their interest does
not stray, because they do not know " what comes next."
And their curiosity—that essential commodity for good
learning—helps their minds to concentrate on what is
happening, and therefore on the language. Thus the meaning
is clear to them, without explanation or translation, and it
is so bound up with a complex of action, feeling and language,
that the new patterns of words and meanings are firmly
impressed on their memories. In brief, the new word in
the new sentence that gives it life is associated with a short
series of actions and speech in some small incident of real
life. Thus the new language is woven by the shuttle of
interest, curiosity and imaginative understanding into the
children's mental life and linguistic habits.

This example, too, of a more complete handling of the
Direct Method has been analysed in order to show how
thoroughly this method should be handled, and how valuable
the Dramatic Method is when carrying out the principle of
the Direct Method. The example also shows how necessary
it is to go beyond the bald idea of " bond between word and
thing." Two points are important: one, that the new words
are an integral part of a living incident, arising out of it;
and second, they have to be *worked into* the pupils' own
thinking and speaking habits.

So we see that in using this method, the teacher might
begin by saying the names of the things in the classroom,
and by letting the children repeat them; but even at the

beginning he could easily bring these words into close association with some classroom action and routine. For instance, " Where is the chalk ? "—" Where is the duster ? " —" The duster is dirty."—" Clean the board, please."[1] Then after the first few lessons, the words to be taught will need to be brought into some simple incident; for instance, some of them can play a part in the mimed sweeping, dusting, tidying of the room; others into an incident of losing something (chalk, inkwell, knife, money—anything). " Where are they ? "—" Look *in the corners, in the cupboard, on the shelf, in your desks.*" Then, later, more complicated incidents can be arranged: making a school dress, getting the classroom ready for acting a play or for an exhibition of pictures: " Where shall I put this picture ? "—" By the clock, under the clock, between the clock and the window." The task of devising little situations may seem at first not at all easy; but once one begins to make them up, little scenes will soon suggest themselves; and after a few have been worked at, the children will take delight in proposing topics to act. Later, a list of these can be made in a few minutes from the suggestions of a class; and then these can be used according as each fits some situation or lends itself to the expression of a cluster of associated ideas.

We have seen examples of situations lending themselves to the use of particular sentence patterns, *e.g.* pretending to lose something calling for the use of " Where is . . . ? ", and instructions to do certain actions giving rise to the use of the Imperative, *e.g.* " Sweep the floor "—" Dust the shelves." At first, therefore, the inventing of ' situations ' will be easier if, in the planning, situation and sentence pattern are thought of together, as far as possible. Thus,

---

[1] In the first lessons, one should keep to the simple sentence patterns: " Where is (are) . . . ? ", " It is . . ." and to the Imperative.

for instance, the structure " Is it large ? " can be fruitfully practised by using the guessing game, in which the children have to ask questions to find out what the teacher or one of the class is thinking about (or, for younger pupils, is holding hidden behind his back). So, too, the sentence " How many . . . has it ? " can have many repetitions without inattention, if the children have to guess what animal, insect, or fish someone has thought of: " How many legs has it ? "—" How many wings, tusks, toes, hoofs . . . ? " Then can follow the use of the sentence structure: " Is its skin, hair, fur, back . . . rough or smooth ? "—" Is its tail long or short ? "—" Is its body thin or fat ? ", and so on. Thus they practise structure, and increase vocabulary by making use of significant and purposeful language. Therefore language is used to find out something that the speaker really wants to know; as it would be used in real life.

Chapter 5

ORAL EXERCISES

FOR the first two or three years of learning a foreign language most of the oral work should be carefully controlled: that is, pupils not left free to select any words they please, or any grammatical forms or constructions. The control will often be determined by the type of exercise that is to be carried out: for instance, an exercise that requires answers to such questions as " Who is . . . ? ", " Where is . . . ? " or " How many . . . ? " limits the pupils to the use of grammatical forms and constructions: " He is a . . .", " It is in the . . .", " It has . . ." Thus the pupils have a very limited choice of the language elements they know, and therefore the opportunity for mistakes is also limited. This is excellent, for beginners must not be given the chance of using a wide variety of forms and structures; otherwise the door to a wide variety of mistake is open. The proper plan is to introduce new grammar and structure into the course gradually, and to ensure thorough repetition of new elements during the weeks following their introduction. The principle to remember here is that everything that can be done to establish the correct forms, constructions, usages in the mental habits of the pupils must be done; because wrong forms are so difficult to eradicate, and because, in language learning, mistakes always slip in—the door can never be quite shut.

Exercises at first therefore need to be carefully selected in order to ensure that the pupils have not a free choice of grammatical form and structure, that there is ample repetition of the new forms, and that the door is not left wide open for every mistake. It will be readily seen that forms of questions, such as " What is this ? " and " Who is this ? " ensure that the pupils keep to the structure " It (he, she) is a . . .", and that the only changes in grammar are in the pronoun. Similarly, the question form " What is the boy doing ? " requires the pupil to use the same Tense in his answer as he hears in the question. These, therefore, exert some control over the language used by the pupil. But if the question form " Why does the boy climb the tree ? " is introduced before the use of the Simple Present Tense in Subordinate Clauses has been practised, answers will inevitably contain the Progressive form (this having been well taught previously), and the result is: " He is climbing the tree because he is wanting a coconut," or " When he is wanting a coconut, he is climbing the tree." Research into the learning of English has found that the Tense required by a question needs to be checked very carefully, before an exercise is given to a class, to make sure a question does not require forms in the answers that have not been learnt.

There are many other pitfalls for the young learner, unless the teacher guides him cautiously during this early stage. For instance, " What is this made of ? " admits of one structure for the correct answer, and it contains the Tense to be used by the pupil; this question form can then be used copiously at first. But an inexperienced teacher might easily vary the question form by asking " What height is it ? "—" How high is it ? "—" What is its height ? ", or even " What is it like ? " This variety of question form would be too much for most beginners, or even for less gifted pupils later on in the course. At first and with slow pupils the question forms with alternatives or those requiring " Yes " or " No " are safe, e.g. " Is it large or small ? " or

" Is it short ? " Only much later with these pupils should
the question form be " What is it like ? "; and much later
still " Tell us something about the . . ." Only when pupils
have mastered a number of sentence forms, and can use them
correctly, should they be called upon to choose from a
number of possible forms and structures.

The principle in organizing the material at first should be:
question forms to contain the Tense, Number and as far as
possible the vocabulary that should be used in the answers.
The method should give very thorough practice with each
new structure, first with only one type of structure in an
exercise, and later with two types, and then later still with
mixed types; though this exercise must be postponed even
later still for backward pupils.

This continual practice with one, and then with two,
sentence types may become monotonous, for there are limits
to the number of times that one can profitably ask " What
is this ? " But variety and attention can be secured by
altering the context: beginning with things in the classroom,
then things on a farm, in a market, in the forest, at a garage,
in a post office, at a carpenter's bench, in a shop, a bank,
a hospital, in a busy street, and so through all the places that
children know and have visited. Thus very copious practice
can be obtained by using the same structures in many very
different kinds of situation. This variety will nearly always
produce intelligent responses from a class.

During the next stage, when reading has begun, good
language practice can be obtained by questioning on the
text. The text then will control vocabulary, structures,
grammar and ideas. Provided the passages through the
Reader[1] are carefully graded, with a very slow increase of

---

[1] A capital letter is used throughout for Reader meaning the book, to
distinguish the word from reader, the person.

difficulty, a teacher need only select his question forms carefully, and sufficient control over the language will be exerted by the text. He must be careful, however, to see that his questions ask only for details that are expressed in the text. Each question must require the pupil to use the words, the grammar and the structure in the text. For instance, " The little girl is feeding her goat." Question: " What is the little girl feeding ? " Answer (at first): " The little girl is feeding her goat." Thus the new words and the sentence pattern are practised, and with very little chance of a mistake. A little later the pupils can answer: " She is feeding her goat," and then, perhaps much later: " Her goat," because they should be well practised in using the sentence patterns of natural colloquial language as well as the complete sentence form. Towards the end of the school course no pupil should be made to spin out fully complete sentences when native speakers of the language would use only a phrase or a single word.

This kind of questioning controls the pupils' answers perfectly: it allows only such mistakes as are due to carelessness and inattention. Furthermore, it can be graded in difficulty to keep pace with the pupils' progress. For instance, it may begin by requiring an answer that is to be found in the Object of the sentence: " What was she feeding ? "—" Her goat "; or in the Subject: " Who was feeding her goat ? " In the next step forward the answer required can be an Adverbial Phrase: " Where was the man going ? ", asked on the sentence in the text: " The man was going to his farm." The next step is " What was the boy doing ? ", asked on the sentence: " The boy was carrying sticks "; where the whole Predicate is to be selected for the answer; then the answers select Predicates containing Phrases: " He was carrying a bucket on his head." Thus the answers required can be gradually longer and longer.

The point here to note particularly is that at this early stage, the question must ask only for what is expressed in words. It must not ask for what can be surmised or ' gathered ' from a sentence, for the pupils are not yet ready for that kind of questioning. The reason for keeping strictly to the details in the text is that the objective here is to give the pupils practice in careful reading and in using the language correctly, impelling them to note the correct structures and grammar by encouraging them to look closely at the text each time to find the answers. This kind of questioning, that asks only for details in the text, we have called " Stage One Questions." It is dealt with more fully later, since it is such a valuable method for training pupils in precise comprehension of what they read.

Question Sequences. At the end of the first year, or early in the second, the Question Sequence method can be started, though with young pupils who are not quick in learning, it might be postponed until later on. In this method, the questions " Where is . . . ? "—" When is . . . ? "—" Why is . . . ? " are asked on every possible occasion, and always in the same order. This helps the pupils to get ready their answers, as they know what is coming; thus many more of them can have some language practice because there are no delays. Quick answering provides more practice, therefore there should be no waiting if a pupil cannot answer; the next pupil must be asked. This short exercise can be completed very quickly because children soon learn to have their answers ready, when the first question is asked: " Where does Ama go to buy food ? ", and so the other questions can be run through immediately: " When does she go ? "—" Why does she go ? " Then, a few sentences later: " Where did the boy go in the lorry ? "—" When did he go in it ? "—" Why did he go to the garage in the lorry ? " Then later: " Where was the accident ? "— " When was there an accident ? "—" Why was there an accident ? "

Action Chains. This exercise would normally come at a later stage than the above, perhaps in the third year of English, though earlier with older pupils. It consists of a number of actions that follow one after the other in a linked series; they are first performed by the teacher, who says at each point what he is doing. Then the pupils do the actions in small groups, the sentences being said in chorus by one of the small groups sitting down, or in turn by each pupil, or by the ones who are doing the actions. For instance, let us take the Boiling Water Action Chain: " I am filling the pot with water . . . I am now carrying it home . . . I am now putting it on the fire . . . Now it is boiling." If a real pot is used, all the better, as the simplest real object, however commonplace, makes such a difference to the active participation of the class in the lesson—much more than would be imagined by anyone who had not seen the difference.

This simple form of the Boiling Water Action Chain is designed for the younger pupils; the older ones would need a fuller version, which might bring in the actions of finding the pot, emptying it, cleaning it, and then going off to the river, well or water-tap, and so on. Thus it can be seen that the exercise can be adapted to the progress of a class and to their vocabulary, because the same topics can be used for young or older pupils, or for slow or quick ones. All one needs to do is to bring in more and more detail, the quicker or older the pupils are.

To begin with, the incidents that the Action Chain exercise makes use of can hardly be too simple or too well known; for instance, the everyday event of a boy returning home from school would be a good one: " When I arrive home, I always greet my parents . . . then I put my books on the table . . . then I take off my school uniform and put on my cloth " (or whatever the boy normally wears at home—in the Gold Coast it will be his ' cloth '). We see here that the exercise is being used to give practice in the use of the Present Simple Tense, with the habitual notion that the Tense expresses explicit in the ' always.' For the younger ones we can have ' getting up in the morning,' ' going to school,' ' collecting firewood '; and for the older pupils: marketing, making bread, pounding fufu. For still older ones the more interesting events of catching a chicken and getting it ready for the pot, or hunting a bush-rat, killing a snake, or bathing the baby would be productive of a closely connected series of actions and sentences.

Later on in the course, when Subordinate Clauses have been practised, the same incidents could be used for a time in order to leave minds free for making up longer sentences, for instance, " whenever I arrive home after a day at school, I always greet my parents politely; then I untie my books and put them ready on the table. I take off my school clothes and hang them up; then I put on my cloth because I like to go out and sit in the compound."

Action Chain exercises are particularly useful as ' drill ' exercises, to get some Tense, Pronoun or Preposition used many times; but their special value is that grammatical forms can be used plentifully in sentences that express something real to the children, instead of in sentences that express unreal events, such as " The boy fell down ", " The teacher spoke quickly ", " The boy kicked the ball." Sentences like these, in isolation and divorced from all the reality of a living scene, have little power to stir language learning abilities to activity; they but touch the surface mechanically.

Action Chains are also valuable because they give language practice which has a high degree of correctness. Mistakes will nearly always be few, for the actions control the expression, and the language cannot get tied up with all sorts of difficulty. Also, once the exercise is understood by a class, the pupils will begin to correct each other whenever a sentence comes in the wrong order, or a language mistake appears: this again raises the standard of correctness. There is an added gain: the pupils are using the language independently of the teacher, both of his help and of the lead he gave at first, for soon they themselves can make up the series of actions as well as the sentences to express them. Then, if the teacher stimulates them to do more and more of the correcting, he can raise the general standard of correctness and make the class responsible for maintaining it. This is a fine ideal to work for; it makes the teacher's work so much more interesting and enjoyable, and it makes it easier for him, because pupils who are keen and alert learn so much more quickly than those who have to be driven.

There is, too, the advantage of using exercises of this type that the meaning of words can be easily demonstrated, thus avoiding the use of translation; and the meaning can be demonstrated so clearly and certainly. Therefore the pupils remember the new language better than if the meanings were shown in separate sentences or in isolated words. It is easier to remember the whole series of actions and sentences because each one leads on naturally to the next. This is a great help to the slower pupils, for they need not worry about their next sentence, when someone is carrying out the actions in front of the class. Therefore the slower ones make good progress, and are not left further and further behind the rest of the class.

It has not perhaps been realized that work like this is the proper training and preparation for free composition. For example, a teacher asks a pupil what he usually does when he wakes up in the morning. The pupil answers: " I get up." The next boy is asked: " What do you do next ? ", and the answer is: " I put on my cloth," and so the class makes up sentences that are connected in idea and all in their right order, or nearly so. Thus, as this work goes on, the pupils gradually learn to speak with their facts and ideas in a good order, because they have such thorough practice in keeping always to the order in which their everyday actions are carried out, which naturally they all know. Investigation of children's written compositions has shown that teaching pupils to write with facts and information in a good order is not at all easy; but constant practice with Action Chains, oral and then written, will no doubt overcome this difficulty.

Action Chains will be useful in the composition course to bridge the gap between single sentences and a connected passage. For example, the teacher need only give the topic of the main action (such as making a catapult), if his class has had good Action Chain practice, and the pupils will begin composing the sentences which, though not always linked by connecting words, make up a connected narrative or description. He has then only to suggest the use of some Conjunctions and Relative Adverbs, and the exercise will lead on easily to some very simple story-telling or descriptive paragraphs. This result is most valuable, because in story-telling the fullest use of language is practised, the language has obvious and easily understood meanings, and it is used for a natural and real purpose.

The use of Action Chains leading on to description and simple stories, helps in a very simple and easy way to remedy another weakness in speaking and writing: namely, the bringing in of a fact, idea, or opinion, that is irrelevant to the subject of a piece of composition. This is a very common fault, but in Action Chains there is no real possibility of pupils introducing irrelevant matter. By expressing the actions that they themselves have done many times, and by being criticized by each other for the slightest deviation from the series of actions which would actually be carried out in real life, pupils learn to keep to a single connected topic; and that is a signal achievement for some pupils.

These Action Chains also tie pupils down to precise details, and so teach them to write clear descriptions. Consequently, at a later stage, they are very much less likely to indulge in the vague, woolly kind of writing that is so prevalent in the work of older pupils, and which is more certain than anything else to blunt the edge of good thinking. By impelling pupils to express precise details, Action Chains help them to think simply and clearly; and plenty of practice in making and expressing simple and precise actions trains their minds to think precisely. Then by stimulating a class to achieve a fine precision of action—neat bodily movement and delicate finger action—a teacher can foster a finer precision of language, and therefore of thought. This is a most valuable result, for when pupils have been trained to reach such standards of thought and expression, they will be able to make a contribution that is of much value to the community—in medicine, veterinary science, agricultural research, optical work, engineering, health service and in all other kinds of work especially requiring clarity and precision of thought, language and action.

C

Chapter 6

THE CHORUS METHOD

THE Chorus Method dates back to the days of mechanical ' rote learning,' and of enormous classes and small staffs, and to the days when it was believed that such learning was education. The method was the main one in use, and perhaps in many schools the only one; but now it is much less widely used. Nevertheless repetition in chorus is a useful and economical method of giving oral practice in a foreign language. In teaching large classes it is a necessary, not an alternative, method. We might remind ourselves here that children learn to speak by imitating, and that this is a natural and legitimate way of acquiring a skill in language, and good chorus work can be achieved only by good imitating.

Unfortunately, too many teachers in the past have used the Chorus Method inefficiently, and have put up with mechanical humdrum repetitions; and they have often allowed their pupils to shout in chorus so loudly and inattentively that mistakes have been repeated every time. This has usually been possible under the cover of the noise, but sometimes because a teacher paid no attention to what was being bawled out. The method is therefore now in disrepute, and deservedly so.

Careful observation during research into learning English has discovered that many of the sentences that are repeated in chorus by a class very often contain mistakes that a teacher does not hear. Frequently, too, some of the sentences bear little resemblance to the model given by the teacher, and some of them make no sense at all. How effective, then, is this practice in speaking that the children are having? When English children repeat incorrect English sentences in chorus, no very great harm is done, though time is wasted; but when incorrect sentences are repeated over and over again by children learning a foreign language, especially one that will be the medium of instruction, then the harm is great: they are learning to use the instrument incorrectly.

The root cause of this misuse of the method is not in the method itself, nor in the inability of the children to imitate accurately: it is in the general conditions often prevailing in a classroom and in the inefficient handling of the method. We all know what the general conditions of a classroom often are: the children are not really attending sharply to what the teacher has said—they are hot and tired, they have heard all that before, and more often than not, there is no need to attend! They can quite well shout out something; they have heard a word or two, and so some of it is right; but there is no exact check on what they shout out. There is plenty of noise, they can easily escape notice; if they make some sounds and move their lips, their teacher does not know that they are not saying the sentence he gave them. In fact, because of the noise it is usually quite impossible to detect mistakes or to know that the pupils are not repeating the sentence perfectly correctly. The consequence of all this is, of course, that mistakes are well drilled in and incorrect usages are successfully learned. And the method is doing harm, not good; and it is not surprising that many teachers will not use chorus repetitions at all.

It can hardly be disputed that chorus work very often encourages incorrect English; for instance, spellings such as ' flus ' for ' fruits,' and ' raing ' for ' raining,' that have been found in written work, were traced to undetected mispronunciations in chorus work. So, too, when a teacher tries to teach ' good oral expression ' (that is, the use of tone and emphasis to bring out the meaning), this will be unsuccessful if a class shouts all together without attending to what they are saying. For it is almost impossible for him to improve the mechanical repetitions, the dull, level tones, the unchanging pace and heavy equal stresses in this unhappy and ugly caricature of what language can be. When this goes on year after year the result is disastrous: the pupils become less and less interested, mistakes increase, and the standards of pronunciation and correctness get lower and lower as the chorus repetitions are continued.

But the Chorus Method at its best is an excellent method for getting language practised at a high level of correctness and expressiveness. The secret is for the teacher to control it, organizing the class and the speaking, and carrying out the work in a special way. This special way is described in detail because this is one of the few methods which should be followed closely, if the speaking practice is to be profitable in its results. Most language teaching methods, however, should be adapted to the abilities of the pupils, and used in different ways to extend their powers.

There are six points in this method to be noted: the first two being essential for success. The first is that only small sections of the class speak in chorus at one time, not the whole class; and the second, even more important, is that the sentences in chorus must always be spoken *softly*.

The size of the section of a class called upon to speak in chorus should not be more than a quarter of the class; for instance, the section might consist of the pupils who are grouped in one column of desks. For fine work and the highest standards, half this number would be best. By having small groups, a teacher can urge each group, if he wishes, to improve on the speaking of the previous one, and in this way help his pupils to speak better. He is able to hear mistakes and to note whose pronunciation is below the level of the others. When groups say their sentences quietly, the teacher is able to hear each individual; and each pupil, knowing that he can be heard, tries to speak correctly. He knows, too, that he must listen carefully to the model sentence, otherwise he will be called upon to repeat it by himself. Then, because every pupil is trying, repetitions bring about improvement. Of course, the teacher must say each sentence very carefully and quietly, for that helps the pupils to say theirs better; and he will need to check his pupils when they raise their voices, as they will at first in the old fashion. This quiet work ensures attention and some effort to speak correctly, and also the participation of every pupil. It also does not interrupt the work of classes in neighbouring rooms, or in the same one, where accommodation is limited.

The next two points are also necessary, if complete success is to be achieved: a high standard must be demanded, and the teacher must listen intently to detect faults. It is not too much to say that unless a teacher works hard and with determination to get the repetitions spoken perfectly, it would be better not to use the method at all. Because if he does not give his full attention to it and is not determined to exact a high standard, the repetitions will get slack, the pupils will not try hard enough, and so their pronunciation will not improve, and mistakes will appear.

What can he do to exact a high standard? He could comment often on each performance: " Not quite correct. Listen again."—" Better; but not yet good enough. Try again."—" Better; nearly right this time."—" Very good indeed "; and so on. He could play one group against another, if he likes that way of stimulating each group to better efforts. He could say a sentence very distinctly and then repeat it at normal speed, and can try to have it spoken with colloquial speed and tone. But one of his best techniques will be to use high praise when a really satisfactory standard has been achieved by a group: " Now *that* sounded nearly like a group of English boys speaking. Well done ! " He would then leave the class feeling confident in their own abilities—and that is always a good thing, if rightly deserved. He may even leave a class feeling that their efforts could have been better, and that the best they were capable of had not been achieved. But whatever he does, he must not give up trying to raise the standard. Then when he thinks a class has done its best, strange as it may seem, he should raise the standard and again try to get his pupils to achieve this new level. The better they speak, the more he may demand from them—and the more exacting he can be ! The best teaching is not weak and easily satisfied; it is strict and exacting. Pupils nearly always respect and admire such teaching; and when they are grown up, they look back on it with pride and gratitude—and with affection for their hard taskmaster.

But to get good results, it is essential to detect carelessness, faults, and mumbling. The teacher has to listen intently to the speaking, for when pupils are speaking in chorus, that is not one of the occasions when he can lean back and relax: he must try to detect who is speaking incorrectly or lazily. If he does not find out who is lowering the standard the general level will fall. If at first he makes those who put little effort into the work say the sentences again by themselves, then most of the pupils will try harder and will give more attention in order to avoid being picked out: thus the standard is maintained. But it is no good leaving this detection of carelessness or incorrectness until later on: it must be started in the very first lesson with this method, then later, it will not be needed so much, and perhaps only occasionally.

The next point to consider is where a teacher should stand. In most kinds of oral lesson the teacher should stand away from his class, right in front or well behind the class; in a position where he can see all of the pupils, and so that they all know that they can be seen by him. For chorus work, however, it is usually better for him to stand close to each group in turn as they speak, or by the side of each group in turn. If he does this he will hear slight inaccuracies of pronunciation better, and also each pupil will know that he can be heard: this helps them to attend to the model sentence and to what they are saying. Attention and effort ensure success in learning.

It is also often better for the teacher not to look at the children while they are speaking (contrary to the customary best practice); but to concentrate solely on listening. He will hear better if he does this, and then the children will give even more care to what they are saying, for they will know what he is doing. All this is necessary because it is so very important that bad habits of pronunciation should not persist, and because it is not at all easy to keep chorus speaking up to a high level of excellence. Finally, the teacher should give good praise for really excellent speaking, and to the backward pupils for marked improvement, never forgetting how encouragement stimulates the efforts of young learners—and of older pupils, too, as we all know from first-hand experience.

In this description of chorus work, we have in mind only the speaking in chorus of single words, single sentences, and, with older pupils, two or three connected sentences in which the elements of tone, rhythm and pronunciation have to be practised. Therefore we have not referred at all to the speaking of verses or poems in chorus; and for a good reason. The speaking of verse in chorus cannot usually have good results unless the teacher has mastered the special methods necessary, and unless he is determined to train his class on the very strict lines that are essential for producing good choral verse-speaking. Because, without special methods and determination to achieve high standards, a teacher cannot prevent chorus repetitions of verse from degenerating into a sing-song, automatic chant, alien to the spirit of good verse.

If the speaking of verse is to be undertaken, it will be essential to make sure that the spirit of the poem selected is correctly appreciated, and that the different groups of children work at the problem of expressing that spirit faithfully, discussing their performances, criticizing their enunciation, tone and rhythm. To achieve good results the teacher needs to be extremely critical of all that the groups produce; for it is a difficult task to train even a small group of children to say some verses expressively in chorus, and very difficult to help them to achieve a high standard, unless the pupils have been particularly well trained in speaking poetry by someone with long experience of this work.

If a class cannot achieve a high standard, even with much practice and strict criticism, it would be better to drop this kind of work. Directly it becomes humdrum and dull, then it has failed, and there is no point in flogging the dead horse. Then, either the pupils are tired or have lost heart, or their abilities and those of the teacher are not equal to the task— it is well to be honest in this matter, because it is not everyone who can handle poetry-speaking in chorus with success, in fact, very few people are really successful. Only when the speaking becomes a pleasure to the children, and when it trains them to read poetry aloud with understanding, giving delight to their listeners, should this method of taking poetry and verse be used.

To sum up: chorus work is valuable only if it fosters improvement. For this effort and care are necessary; therefore small groups and quiet speaking are essential. Usually the chorus repetitions should last only for a few minutes in order to keep attention and effort up to concert pitch, without using persuasion or commands. To exact a high standard, the teacher has to insist on more and more correctness in each repetition, and on an increasingly exact imitation of his good model; and he will have to exert himself, and concentrate his attention and listening if he is to secure improvement. If he does all this, and shows that he is always resolutely determined to get the best out of the class, the pupils will learn to take a pride in their speaking of the foreign language: then a class becomes lively, keen to do well and fully interested in its own progress and in ways of improving the chorus speaking. Then is the time for the teacher to raise the standard and to demand more from them. He will soon realize from their ready response that they enjoy the continual struggle for perfection. Then they will produce well-pronounced and expressive language, spoken with the natural intonation and rhythm of the native speaker of the language.

Chapter 7

MIMING AND CLASSROOM PLAY-ACTING

IT is not commonly known that much of the language teaching that goes on everywhere does not teach pupils to speak the language. The main reason for this is that the words and most of the sentences that pupils pore over so laboriously, or that are drummed into them so conscientiously, are ' book ' words and sentences: they do not arise from any real-life situation. They are not used as real language is used, because nobody is communicating anything, nobody is enquiring, commanding, persuading, informing, confiding, or using the language for any purpose, intention or wish to speak or write. Nearly all the language that most learners try to master is the surface language of sound and dictionary meanings: it is not heard and studied as a language that fulfils a living need to express feeling or wish or other impulse, such as one expresses in real life almost whenever one speaks. Consequently this language has no roots in a human desire to communicate, and no living sap flows into it from a human mind and will. This ' book ' language therefore has not the full force of a living word which is spoken because someone *wants* to speak. The consequence of this is that the language makes little impression on pupils' minds; and they therefore easily forget most of it. But if the language of real life were to be used habitually in the teaching of a foreign language, pupils would learn it more quickly and more thoroughly.

We see, too, that the exercises in an English course require the reproduction, sentence-completion or re-expression of ideas in the Readers (necessary at first).

This is satisfactory as far as it goes; but much more is needed, because a flat, unvaried diet of that kind of work inevitably leads to more and more dependence on the book. The pupils think of what is in the book, whenever they have to use the language, and try to remember what they have seen there. They do not often enough have to make use of the language without reliance on their books, and thus they learn a language that is tied to their Reader. We see then that the new language is not being used frequently enough as a natural medium of expression and communication, as in real life, and therefore most of the pupils cannot acquire a free, fluent and useful command of the new language. The remedy for this is simple.

Every teacher of languages should devise ways and methods of getting the new language used as it is in real life, that is, language that performs some useful purpose: to ask for something, to enquire about somebody, to tell somebody something, to tell someone to do something. These are the normal purposes of spoken language, though at times we use it for less direct purposes, for example, to fill in time until a senior arrives, or to cover up one's shyness in company, or to make friendly contact with a stranger. In real life we use language because we are interested in something, because we have enjoyed something, because we are unhappy and want sympathy. Or we may use speech to overcome loneliness, or to help others, or to get something for ourselves. Thus in real life there are four driving forces: usefulness, purpose, wanting, emotion. These make expression in language necessary to us, infusing our use of words with the urgency of our needs for satisfaction and fulfilment.

Now for learners during the early years, a new language can have these expressive powers only in dramatic work, or in Direct Method teaching that dramatizes everyday incidents and happenings. And there can be no doubt that the Dramatic Method provides practice in the use of a new language of such quality and completeness that no other kinds of exercise and method can equal.

The full value of the Dramatic Method has, however, rarely been properly understood. It is particularly valuable because it gives some semblance of reality to the language learned in the classroom. It therefore saves repetitions and learning from being purely mechanical, and reveals to the minds of the learners the meanings of the sentences. When a teacher introduces some little by-play, some pretended haste or excitement, some humour or feigned anger, then a fuller reality and significance is given to the words and to the expression of what he is doing. He can mime his hurry to catch a bus, putting on a hat, collecting his things and dashing out; or he can show that he is expecting a visitor, and when he opens the door politely (and perhaps somewhat pompously), there is no one there. All he has to do is to suggest briefly by his actions some simple social incident, with perhaps a touch of humour, and then the language will have its full purpose: expression and communication, as in real life. The pupils then are learning to listen to and use the living language, and are not just repeating sentences that they have read in their books, which for them are often shadow expressions and verbal formulæ.

The Dramatic Method is also valuable because actions can make the meanings of words clearer and more certain than can explanations or descriptions; and so the mind remembers them better. Translations, explanations, definitions, are but paraphrases, mere verbal equivalents, of a word's essence, its meaning. Whereas the actions of a living person can precisely and vividly express the full meaning of a word in the context which gives it its role and significance. Actions, therefore, leave an exact impression on the senses and a permanent record of the meaning on the minds of the learners.

We can be certain, therefore, that when a teacher opens the door and says: " I am opening the door slowly," the pupils know that he is expressing just what he is experiencing. They see the physical event that is expressed by the words ' am opening the door '; they see it as real, taking place before their eyes, and they perceive and understand the meaning of the words in a living real existence; and so this meaning is not only more certain, but also more clear-cut, and more definite. Then, because it is not merely a dictionary meaning, but sharp in outline, it is attended to, and therefore afterwards more readily recalled to mind. Explanations in words are theoretical; actions are practical —they are part and parcel of reality.

In all dramatic work, even in the simplest dramatic dialogue, the meanings of words and sentences are clearer and more definite than they are in nearly all other kinds of language practice. The general understanding of what is happening in some little everyday incident that is being acted helps the duller pupils to grasp immediately the meanings of what is said. The characters, the place and cause of their meeting, the expressive tones and rhythms they use, their gestures, as well as the pupils' knowledge of what would be said in real life, all help the duller ones to understand the meaning of the words. Many teachers and heads of schools suppose that the Dramatic Method is used in order to make the work interesting and pleasant. They have not perceived its true purpose: it is certainly not used in order to make the work pleasanter and more effortless for inattentive and lazy pupils. It is used because it helps pupils to understand the language, and because then the language is used as in real life. It is really an essential method for teaching foreign languages.

All this may appear complicated and to demand too much from the child; but it can be quite easy and within the capabilities of every one in the class, even in the first year of learning a new language. We may have referred here to some of the deeper aspects of the psychology of language by analysing in a simple way the role of purpose in the use of language in real life; but in teaching, the simpler and the more familiar the dramatizing is at first, the better. So then the teacher may select the simplest everyday incidents of the life that the children know and the commonplace routines that they are accustomed to, for these are the best material for beginners to work upon. For instance, the meeting of two friends, a girl returning home after visiting an aunt, a boy packing his kit for a cycling trip, two sisters selling fruit in the market, a mother taking her baby to the clinic. A few simple sentences can be suggested by the class, and some of these can be corrected and perhaps then written down; but not by the youngest pupils who have not long been writing the new language, or for whom writing is troublesome, because then the writing would hold up the speaking, and so it should be postponed. When the action has been proposed and discussed, the pupils in pairs or threes or fours can either perform the incident in mime or act it with dialogue, each group in turn. After a few lessons like this, many classes will choose their own incidents or will produce different versions of a selected one.

We can examine the use of action, mime and acting in the classroom under the following heads: (*a*) the use of gesture and mime, (*b*) action and speech, (*c*) acting and classroom play production.

(*a*) **The Use of Gesture and Mime.** To summarize what has been said on this topic: gesture is one of the most effective instruments of the language teacher; he can point, beckon, show direction, indicate movement—" Sit, Stand, Come here, Go "—and he can emphasize this or that. All these meanings can then be taught from the beginning, when it is more difficult to do without the mother tongue. Then when the teacher says the words to express what his gestures have indicated, the pupils understand immediately. At this early stage the pupils too can use the gestures, and practise the words with their additional help. Even when the words are well known, the gestures should be continued, because it is useful to make the use of gesture a natural habit in learning languages.

Physical action is a more effective aid in forming linguistic habits than most teachers realize. We must remember that the brain is only " The Clearing House," " The Exchange " and " Co-ordinator," and not the sole originator of thought, feeling and language; and one's mental life is a function of the whole. Gestures, therefore, should be used throughout oral work, for they are such a quick and clear way of conveying meaning that no language teacher can afford to neglect their use.

Gesture is an especially easy way of teaching opposites in meaning, and of teaching these early, for example: " This-That "; " Into—Out of "; " Near—Far "; and then with more expressive movement: " Give-Take "; " Come-Go "; " Raise-Lower "; " Open-Shut." It is a good plan to teach opposites together, because it is so easy; though they should not be presented as a series of opposites in a double list; but incidentally, when one word of a pair occurs, the other can just as well be taught, too.

Later, gesture is a valuable way of making distinctions between meanings that are similar. For instance, gesture can make clear differences between " I knock on the door," " I bang the door," " I bang on the door," and " I tap on the door "; or between " I rap on the table " and " I thump on the table "; or between " I knock in a nail " and " I screw in a hook "; or between " I pounce on the chicken " and " I grab at the chicken " (pupils may not note a difference between " grab at " and " pounce on," but they can soon see the difference it makes to the chicken). The special value of gesture for distinguishing similar meanings is that it makes clear the precise meaning in a way that children can remember, for the eye is often a more faithful servant than the ear. We may remind ourselves here that attending to precise meanings is the way to learn to think clearly and to learn to appreciate great literature.

From gesture that reveals the meanings of single words, the teacher can soon pass on to mime all kinds of action: how people walk, speak, write, run; and so teach first single Adverbs, then Adverbial Phrases, then Clauses; or first single Adjectives (fat, thin, high, smooth), then Adjectival Phrases (with a heavy load, nearest the door, the man in blue), and even many Nouns (policeman, fisherman, carpenter). In this way very many words that cannot easily be shown in pictures, or when no pictures are available, can be taught easily and precisely and with the enjoyment of the class.

(*b*) **Action and Speech.** Later, action and speech will provide the best exercise for practising the use of the language as it is heard and spoken in everyday life. At first the teacher might begin by imitating some complicated action, such as washing and ironing clothes, or preparing some food for the pot, or making a toy of some sort. As he does this the class puts into words what he is doing, if they can; if not, he can say them. Thus a continuous piece of spoken English is obtained. The pupils could use this and similar pieces for their written work, if they are not quick learners, or have not been learning English for very long. Then they might mime various actions of a similar nature, first in turn and then in groups, and the rest of the class can say what is being done. Next, the class might suggest and discuss other actions, *e.g.* a policeman on traffic control, a lorry driver changing a wheel, a carpenter making a chair, a tailor giving a fitting, a goldsmith weighing gold ear-rings, a girl having her hair done (according to the local fashion), fishermen mending nets or hauling them on shore—whatever is well known to the children, as many of these will be in one area or another. Nearly everyone of the ordinary activities of everyday life in village or town, in farm or market, on the sea-shore or at the water tap or well, will be suitable for this work. There is no lack of subjects which will help to produce good natural English, used correctly and with keen attention.

When a class is allowed to criticize the acting and the speaking, and is encouraged to show how some of the actions can be done more neatly and *truer to real life*, then the class will take pains to do their acting better, and they will enjoy the work more as the standard of performance improves. Then, too, the expression of the improving actions becomes more careful and correct. General progress in learning the language follows when a class is persuaded or spurred on to try to attain to higher standards.

In the next year, little dialogues, conversations between three or four characters, and slightly longer dramatic incidents might begin; for example, two women talking as they go to fetch water or to sell produce from their farms in the market, or two friends meeting after long absence (though the customary excitement should not be too hilarious or a caricature !), a dispute on a lorry, or an argument between lorry-driver and a suspicious policeman, a car break-down, a small crowd growing more friendly during the usual long wait for a bus. In all of these there is plenty of opportunity for bringing in varied and interesting characters. It is usually best to start a class discussing what the characters might say, as that provides some preparation for the dialogue, and improves the use of language; it also gives clearer definition of the speakers, that is, exactly who they are and what they would really say in the circumstances that the class has outlined. Before speaking, too, the class should make suggestions about what the characters could do to show who they are and what is happening.

With a poor class, this planning before speaking and acting must be kept up for rather a long time, as it will be necessary in order to make the method profitable. With many of such classes it is best to ask for suggestions about what the characters will say, so that nobody becomes tongue-tied, and so that the language may be corrected beforehand. At first, some of the dialogue could be written on the board, as this helps to prepare the weaker ones for speaking, and serves as a prompter if they forget what to say when acting. But with good classes, extempore speaking and acting can be started after a few weeks of performing prepared scenes, though some discussion and planning is nearly always best, for otherwise the dialogue might become too free and therefore incorrect.

(c) **Acting and Classroom Play Production.** Naturally this work requires more thorough preparation than the extempore action and dialogue we have been considering. Stories will provide the best material for this somewhat more

ambitious classroom activity. At first, a story might be read
to the class, or one selected from the Reader; then the plot,
action and characters have to be discussed fully in class, and
the work carefully planned. This provides purposeful oral
practice and is just as important from the learning point of
view as the speaking of the parts; it should therefore be
thorough. The class might make suggestions for the action,
etc., and then these should be criticized, and improvements
proposed, unless they are particularly good. It is often best
to have parts of the play performed by one or two groups,
and before going on, to call for improvements again. The
play can then be run through by other groups, the class
being persuaded that the first trials are experimental. Thus
improvement in language follows. It is well to remember,
however, that improvement in language is promoted by
improvement in action: it will not follow usually from
advice, commands or instructions.

Very good classes will soon act scenes spontaneously, and
will make up dialogue as they go along; but usually previous
planning is best, as there is always the problem of incorrectness. However, to start one group acting with very short
preparation, and then to discuss improvements for the other
groups to make is a good way with quick and intelligent
pupils who have had good practice in miming and play-
acting. The method and the plan from day to day must
depend on the ability of the class and their achievements in
earlier work, and also especially on the determination of the
teacher to get constant improvement.

Later the class can dramatize stories from Supplementary
Readers, from history, fables and folk-lore, biography,
travel, exploration and adventure, but always with an eye to
language improvements. Parts of the longer stories can be
done by different groups: there is no necessity for any one

group to do a complete story. Comments and suggestions for improvements should continue, but most of these should at this late stage be directed to improvements that will result in a better use of language, as the aim here is not to produce the plays for the sake of a good performance, but to provide lively and natural language practice. There is one small trick that usually promotes improvement: a teacher should often ask questions about *how* an action is done, *e.g.* " How will the lorry-driver show he cannot find out why his engine won't start ? "—" How can he make it perfectly clear what he is doing ? " Questions of this type compel the children to think more closely about the details of the imaginary scene and the action needed to give rise to language.

When a play is taken from the Reader or from a Supplementary Reader, the story should be read silently, then the teacher should question the class fully about the plot, the characters and the action. This helps the slower pupils to imagine the story more completely and vividly, for these pupils are slow learners usually because their imagination and intelligence are so rarely goaded into activity. After the parts and action have been decided upon, an average class should again read the story through silently, in order to memorize some of the dialogue, or they may write out what they are going to say, if they are able to make up dialogue correctly. Many children can do their acting well enough with the book in their hands; but those who cannot may have to learn some of the dialogue by heart. Even the more skilful pupils should not be allowed to make up dialogue as they go along unless their command of the spoken language is very good.

One word of advice for this kind of work: a teacher should not say " Do this " and " Do that "; he ought to say " How *would* this character do this action ? "—" How

do people usually show surprise ? "—" Think of a woman
cutting off the peel of an orange with a big knife: how does
she do it ?—Show us ! " The reason for this way of leading
the pupils on to think of what happens in real life is that it
stirs their imagination, and so produces more expressive
action and more natural speech. It also develops the pupils'
abilities, especially their imagination, instead of merely
producing better imitated action. We often forget that the
imagination is one of the most valuable helps for language
work, since we make use of it in every walk of life: in
planning, in explaining, in giving instructions, in thinking,
communicating and in carrying out our daily tasks, clerical
or manual, if we do all these intelligently. And the more
precisely and appropriately we use our imaginations, the
better shall we carry out all these duties, tasks and
undertakings.

Thus we see that some skill in handling the Dramatic
Method is most valuable. It can help pupils in the early
stages to learn so thoroughly that success later is practically
assured; for then all later learning has a firm basis of solid
linguistic knowledge and habit, instead of the shifting sands
of half-perceived and half-remembered ' book ' words and
sentences, without situation or purpose or any power of
communicating anything. The interpretation of meaning by
action is essential for beginners: all young teachers and old
teachers of the young should remember this, and should
deliberately practise the art of mime. It is one of the most
valuable secrets of the art and craftsmanship of language
teaching.

Chapter 8

FIRST STEPS IN WRITING THE NEW LANGUAGE

IN countries where children rarely use pen or pencil at home during their earliest school years, and where they do not write much in their mother tongue at school, the written work in the new language needs to be carefully graded. But in countries where children handle chalks, paint-brushes, pencils and pens at an early age, the writing of the new language can proceed along the lines of their writing of the mother tongue, and at much the same rate of progress, unless the lettering is new to them, as it is, for instance, to Arab children learning French or English, and to most children in India who are unaccustomed to the Roman script.

The beginnings of writing a new language should normally be reproduction (or transcription as it is sometimes called). It is perhaps best for the children to copy what has been written on the board, as then the formation of the written letters will be learnt without special lessons. Whereas, if the children copy something from print, special lessons on script or cursive writing may have to be given. Perhaps the ideal thing is to use the old-fashioned ' copybooks,' if they can still be obtained.

This first step in writing should make use of sentences that have been practised orally. No new words, new grammar or new constructions should be included, because in copying sentences from a blackboard there is already almost too much for the weaker pupils to attend to and to copy correctly. The task of forming strange and differently shaped letters, of getting these in the same order as those on the board and not leaving out any of the words, is one requiring exact observation. This is not the right opportunity for teaching new words, or even for giving practice in the use of recently learnt sentences.

It may be useful to consider the purpose of reproduction. At this stage it is not merely a mechanical exercise; but has a useful part to play at first in language learning, and therefore it is worth planning to make it really effective. We again remind ourselves that the eye is a good helper in learning; the advantage therefore of copying sentences in writing is that the pupil *must* look at the words. When he has to look at the words on the board carefully in order to copy them the pupil forms mental pictures of these words, inflections and structures; and when he writes them the action enlists the aid of the muscular memory to reinforce the visual.

The second advantage is that the learner has to be actively forming the words and building up the structures of the sentences as he is writing them. Although he is copying a sentence he has to remake it word by word: he is therefore learning sentence structure. And if he has had good practice with these sentences orally, he cannot avoid thinking of their meaning as he completes them. He may even say the meaning over quietly to himself—this perhaps might be encouraged. He thus learns unconsciously, for instance, that the name of the thing that he ' makes,' ' cuts,' ' buys ' or ' digs ' comes after the word expressing the action. So he becomes familiar with the most frequently used sentence patterns; and if he makes a structural mistake of wrong word order, he may perceive that he has altered the sentence. This habit of unconsciously recognizing structure is very important; because so much of the learning and the use of a new language is based on the passive recognition of the patterns. Just as many of us often write down a word in order to see how to spell it, because our eyes ' know ' the spelling by the look of the word, so we master the most commonly used sentence patterns of a new language partly by the look of them, by what is known as their ' Form.'[1] Writing helps us very considerably to acquire this recognition knowledge of a new language.

With linguistically able pupils, who learn without great effort, reproduction need not be carried on for long; but for the slow ones and for children who have had little experience of writing, reproduction should be continued for some time, though, of course, not as the only exercise. If pupils become careless and show no interest in doing it well, it might be given up; though, as it is so useful, the better plan would be to devise ways of making it worthwhile. For instance, the class could copy down conversations, verses or short passages that will be studied a little later on, or that can be used for another kind of exercise. Questions could be copied down that later will be answered, and the beginnings of short stories that later will be completed.

The gradual increase of difficulty previously mentioned can easily be planned: in the first stage, the pupils write down exactly what is on the board. In this work no opportunities for mistakes are given, except those due to carelessness or too rapid observation; though children with poor eyesight will always make mistakes. In the second stage, the children copy down parts of sentences, and then have to complete them themselves. In the third, they have to write down the questions on the board, and then answer them, or

---

[1] The importance of ' Form ' in learning was one of the valuable contributions to education of the *Gestalt* psychology. The idea that learning is quicker and more lasting when what is to be learnt can be seen in a pattern, or more or less fixed ' design,' repeated in different contexts, is particularly valuable for language learning.

they may write down short passages of narrative which later they will fill out and make more exact by the addition of Adjectives, Adverbs and Phrases expressing time, place and manner.

Other kinds of written work can develop from the exercise, when the pupils are ready for them. For instance, variations in a simple story may be made and the addition of some descriptive details. If this is successful, the variations made by the pupils can be increased until sufficient practice in filling out a story or in re-telling stories has been given. This should lead on naturally and easily to story-telling, which needs careful preliminary training before the full task is attempted. Thus a gradual transition to more difficult work is planned, and so the slower pupils do not find the later work too much for them.

We must now go back to the Sentence Completion Exercise, which has also grown out of reproduction, and plan a course of increasing difficulty, using this exercise. At first, the parts of the sentence to be added by the children should be Objects, Adverbs and Adjectives; then Adverbial Phrases. These will be the easiest to begin on. In the first few lessons, at least, it will be necessary to run through the exercise orally before writing begins. The purpose of this is to give as much help as possible to the class in order to have the written work done correctly, and not to allow too much freedom of choice. After these simple beginnings have been well practised, longer completions may be demanded; but, again, suggestions should first be discussed orally, especially with slow classes. With a very good class, the pupils could be asked to explain why some suggestions were rejected; they should be able to see where incorrect structure, absurd idea, unintelligibility, untrue fact, etc. account for rejection. This gives a sharp stimulus to the quickest pupils, and will urge them to make up better sentences.

Later, whole Predicates can be left blank for the pupils to fill in; but with this type of completion it is best to include an Adjectival or Adverbial Phrase in a sentence in order to give a clue that makes clear what Predicate would be appropriate. For instance, " After buying petrol, the driver . . ." will more likely be completed correctly and sensibly than " The driver . . ." So the sentences to be completed will be similar to " The policeman, directing the traffic . . ."—" During the robbery, a weaver in the next compound . . ." It will be noted that a given clue will reduce the number of likely mistakes: the pupils also have some practice in thinking and in drawing very simple conclusions.

We may note that by making suggestions orally before the writing begins, the pupils have opportunities for using their own ideas and language: thus their individual needs for expression are being attended to in a very simple way. This is profitable, for the pupils are then being prepared for the next long step they must take: the step to ' free ' composition, which demands much from them and requires a good command of the language. Exercises that give good language practice, and also provide some preparation for a next step forward should always be noted: thus gradual progress can be planned and a steady march forward made possible.

Question and Answer Exercises can also be graded. At first the question will contain the words and structure that are needed in the answer; next they contain the words but not the Tense; later, the questions may call for almost entirely new sentences. For example, the first question form might be: " Where have you been ? "; " How many

brothers has your sister ? "; " Where is your home ? "
Next the type of question might be: " When do your
holidays begin ? "; " Do you like playing football ? ";
" What time do you get up in the morning ? " Then,
several weeks later for slow pupils: " What do you do on
Saturdays ? "; " What is your school like ? "; " How do
you clean a cooking-pot ? "

Before going on to ' free ' composition, a class should
practise writing short explanations, almost any paragraph
that is not too simple may be chosen for this work. The
paraphrasing should be run through orally, and should at
first keep exactly to the facts and thought of the paragraph.
Later, simple details may be added and a free version of a
paragraph produced. It would be very valuable if the pupils
could try to make the passage more exact by their additions
to it, for instance, making a description more detailed, or
the simple background of a short anecdote more complete,
or by including reasons, motives, causes. The characters
and events will then be more fully understood. This kind
of work should help the pupils to think more precisely and
write more exactly—which is so difficult to train children
to do.

The guiding rule for all the written work at first, simple
as this work will be, is that the children should not be urged
to run before they can walk. They must be well practised
in using at first only the words, sentence patterns, and ideas
that they have worked at orally, and in doing the exercises
in their Readers. For the first year or two, they should not
be asked to speak and write on subjects outside their classroom reading and their oral lessons; otherwise they may
lose grip on the structures and grammar that they have
learnt. Too free a use of the simple elements of language
that they have been practising will often produce so many

errors that instability in the use of all they have been learning may result.

With classes of slow or backward pupils, the first step towards a freer use of the language should be for the pupils to make up sentences exactly on the pattern of the sentences in their Readers, and based on the ideas expressed in these sentences, while extending them to similar ideas. For instance, the model sentence in the book, " My father often goes fishing," might give rise to " My brother often goes hunting "—" His uncle often goes shooting." There is little chance of these pupils making any mistakes if they keep to the same Tense and Number as in the model. Soon they should be able to go on to " Some men are digging a trench by the road," and then write such sentences as " Some farmers are clearing the ground near the village." But thorough questioning on all the reading they do, ample oral work with well-known everyday topics and the language exercises in the Readers should soon get even these pupils far beyond these simple beginnings.

The next step in the writing programme might also make use of the paragraphs in the Reader; for the subject-matter and the language will provide useful material for the writing of short paragraphs. For instance, having read about a market in Egypt, India or France, the children should then discuss the market they know, saying what they do and see and hear there (and perhaps smell there, too: smells of spices, frying fish, frying plantain, ripe mango—and animal smells !). The lesson in their Reader should supply them with all the words and expressions that they need to write about these things. Then, *with Readers open*, each pupil writes just what he himself does in the market and sees and hears there; and he turns to the book often to make sure he is using correct language, or to look for any word or expression he is not quite sure about. Any new words needed by the writers, or that are suggested during the oral preparation, will of course have been written on the board, and left there for the children to use in their writing if they wish.

We must deal with a simple point here because its value may be missed. Whenever the children make grammatical or spelling mistakes in sentences that they have copied or adapted from their books or the blackboard, they should correct them themselves. There can be no valid excuse for such mistakes. They will learn the correct forms if they have to alter the sentences in their own books. Careful habits in using language need to be fostered on every occasion, especially during the early years.

In this kind of work, the oral preparation and previous work on the passage in the book will help the pupils to select and express what they wish to write. If then there are very many mistakes, most of them will be due to carelessness and inattention, or to insufficient and too superficial oral preparation beforehand, though sometimes they may be due to the ideas being too difficult for the pupils. On the other hand if the slower ones follow the book too closely, that will not matter at first, for they will be having practice in writing correct English, even if they are not being trained to express ideas of their own. These slow pupils should not be pressed to go on quickly from stage to stage in this composition work. " More haste, less speed " applies especially to these pupils in their language learning course.

Chapter 9

THE TEACHING OF GRAMMAR

UNLIKE teachers of the mother tongue, the teachers of foreign languages do not question the necessity for teaching the grammar of a new language. Nevertheless, they have considerable doubts about *how* this grammar should be taught. And sometimes what grammar should be taught is a cause for disagreement. But the problem of what grammar to teach is comparatively simple. Common-sense tells us that pupils learning English must know the Plural forms of common Nouns, such as ' child,' ' penny,' ' fish,' and the commonly used Tense forms of the Verbs they will use. Such items have to be learnt and remembered; though it is much more important that these items should be *used* correctly than that lists of Plural Nouns or Principal Parts of Verbs should be reproduced accurately: to be able to repeat paradigms and conjugations correctly is not the proper purpose of learning grammar.

Many older teachers, who in their youth had to learn the forms of Nouns, Verbs, Pronouns, etc., by rote, often plead for " More Grammar ! " They believe that pupils who come to them now make many more mistakes than their former pupils used to do. There is something to be said for this plea and argument; but there is much more to be said for the view that practice in using the new language should not be held up while pupils are trying to memorize all its commoner forms. For it is useless knowing the forms, if the pupils cannot read a simple story or put together some simple sentences to say what someone is doing.

It is unfortunately true that pupils who learn in the new way, reading simple passages, speaking simple dialogue and writing unaided short easy passages, and in the course of this, picking up some grammar as they go along, do not know with sufficient accuracy the various forms of the words they need and use. But that is mainly because ' drill ' exercises have not been handled efficiently enough, because the grammar exercises based on the reading are insufficient in number and length, and because these are not properly organized in graded steps. In short, exercises hardly ever supply adequate practice in *using* the grammatical forms met with in each lesson. It would have been better, therefore, if the plea had been " Better Grammar Teaching ! " instead of " More Grammar." It is comparatively easy to memorize grammatical forms, but difficult to master the usage of those forms. And it is of no value at all to know all the Tense forms of a Verb, unless one knows also which Tense to use. It is more useful to knòw when to say: " Have you finished that letter ? " and when to say: " Did you finish that letter ? " than to know the Principal Parts of the Verb ' to finish.'

Now, what is this " Better Grammar Teaching " ? Or to vary the enquiry, " How can grammar best be taught ? " To begin with, we should realize that there is not just one way of teaching grammar. Learning lists of Principal Parts of Verbs, or of other forms, is only one way, and any one way is quite insufficient, if the grammar is to be learnt and used correctly. The reason for this is that the grammar to be learnt is so varied in its nature and usage that different ways of teaching it have to be devised, each way suitable for the different kinds of grammar that have to be learnt; for instance, the Plurals of Nouns must be taught in a different way from the use of ' were ' and ' have ' with Plural Subjects.

This point seems to have been entirely disregarded in most language courses.

Thus we see that a teacher must use various types of grammar exercises and various methods in order to give each different type of grammatical form and syntax the practice and application that will be appropriate to it. For instance, there should be instruction, or simple deductive exercises, for learning the main rules for forming the Plurals of Nouns, and adequate practice in using these Plurals in sentences. There must be construction exercises for mastering the use of Relative Pronouns: here imitation rather than deduction should be the method, for so-called rules will give no help. The three main types of exercise—imitation, application, construction—will cover most of the work on grammar. The greater part of the learning should not be listening to explanations by the teacher; but applying what has been learnt by rote or analogy or observation. Most of the necessary grammar, then, will be learnt through the very numerous exercises calling for the construction of sentences, in answering questions that require the use of the grammar to be learnt, and in Completion Exercises.

There is yet another point to be considered in answer to the " More Grammar " demand: when the learners are quite young, almost any instruction on grammar confuses them. It is true that some of the grammar can be made very simple, or a usage may become evident through a large number of easy exercises, when the brighter pupils can deduce the rule, but for the majority this often fails. For the younger pupils, therefore, not " More Grammar," but " More and Better Organized Practice " is the soundest plan. They can, too, be given so much practice in hearing and speaking and reading the language, that they learn much of the grammar without specific instruction. For instance, they become so accustomed to using the Singular after " There is . . ." and the Plural after " There are . . ." that they do not need any instruction about Concord[1] and the so-called agreement in Number of Subject with its Verb.

The way to deal with the learning of the Principal Parts of Verbs, especially the Strong Verbs, is to have some of the commonest learnt by heart, and then, throughout the five or six or more years of learning the language, to call upon individual pupils to give the Principal Parts of a Verb that has occurred in the text that is being studied, or that has been suggested during oral preparation for speaking or writing. This takes only half a minute or so, and if it is made a regular and fairly frequent practice it keeps these forms fresh in the minds of everyone in the class. It is a procedure that used to be widely practised by foreign language teachers in Hungary, and no doubt is still the custom, as it is such a good piece of teaching technique; for pupils are alert and can run through the forms without waiting for instructions; and so very quick revision is achieved with a small expenditure of effort.

The organization of the grammar work has been referred to earlier; it is a subject that is often neglected. The limitation of vocabulary and the controlled infiltration of new words into a language course have held the centre of interest; but the gradual infiltration of new grammar items has not been given the attention that it needs. Little research has been done on it, and there is no consensus of opinion on what should be done, or published results of experience that we can consult. The problem is still awaiting a willing and well-informed worker.

---

[1] Concord in English operates *only* with the Present Tense, the Present Perfect and the Continuous Tenses. It has, therefore, not the importance in English that it has in French and German.

D

The problem is this: " What grammar should be taught in the first year, in the second, the third, and so on; and in what order should the selected items by taught: for instance, the Future Tense before the Present Perfect, or after it ? " It would be a great help to young pupils if we knew whether it would be possible to postpone some apparently necessary grammar until the second or third year, to save the first year from being overburdened with grammatical work. Some suggestions are put forward in the next paragraph; but the pooled experience of many teachers could provide much valuable evidence that would help us to answer these questions.

Parts of this problem, however, will not provoke argument; for instance, Plurals can be learnt as the Nouns are met with, or needed; and at first only those should be learned. The Personal Pronouns in the Subject and Object relations (I—me, he—him, they—them, etc.) will also be needed in the earliest stage. But which should be taught first—the Simple Present Tense or the Continuous Present ? A sound answer to this question can be arrived at by noting the methods used by the teacher: if he uses the Direct Method regularly, then the Present Continuous will be more useful, and he will be able to keep to it for some time. But if he decides to use reading as the main exercise, then the Present Simple can come in much earlier, and will be needed earlier as in: " And the woman said to her daughter, ' When *you go* to the market . . . I *want* you to . . . But if the stranger *comes* to your stall again to-day . . .' " Those who use the Direct Method and who therefore make full use of oral exercises, can often postpone the teaching of the Simple Present until the idea of actions occurring frequently, or as a habit, should be taught, as in: " When I *get* out of bed, I always *roll* up my mat, and then I *put* . . ."

The chief reason for teaching the Present Continuous first is that it is needed to express actions that are being performed in front of a class; whereas the Simple Present is not urgently needed at an early stage. Of course, if a teacher says (as he all too frequently does): " I open the book "—" I look at the clock "—" I walk to the door " *as he does these actions*, then he is teaching the wrong use of the Tense; and he should not be surprised that his pupils' commonest mistake is one of Tense.

We may note, too, that the Continuous Present can be used in a very large number of situations; but the Simple Present cannot. And, to be sure, the disadvantage of having to learn " *I am* speaking, *you are* . . ., *he is* . . ." is not greater than having to puzzle out the use of ' s ' for the Singular Verb (" He works "), and ' s ' for the Plural Noun (" The boys work "), but no ' s ' for the Verb with the Plural Noun. This example shows us that, in planning a course which includes much grammar, the *learning burden* should always be given careful consideration.

There need, however, be no long delay in teaching either of these Tenses, because the difference between an action that a boy is doing now, and an action which he does every day, is not at all difficult to illustrate freely, and no grammatical terms are needed to make the difference perfectly clear; though a great deal of practice will be necessary after the second Tense has been introduced in order to prevent the pupils from confusing the two. Later, still more practice will be needed when the use of the Present Simple in Subordinate Clauses is taught, as in " When he *comes* in, I want you . . .", " If they *go* out before I *return*, you must . . ." The copious practice needed will be in the pupils' using each Tense in very many sentences expressing varied actions in many different situations—not in frequent explanations. Unfortunately, the efficacy of practice in using sentences is not trusted by some teachers, for they imagine that intellectual explanation is more effective in teaching than practice and application; as if learning a language were purely an intellectual affair.

We may note here that at first every sentence containing a Continuous Present should also contain the word ' now,' and every sentence expressing habitual actions should contain the words ' always ' or ' every morning ' or ' every day '; for it is essential that beginners should be distinctly aware of the ' time ' or ' aspect '[1] of the action that is expressed by the Verb. By associating a Tense with a word which exactly expresses the time or aspect of the action, we can help to fix the correct usage of the Tense in the linguistic habits of the pupils. The regular use of an Adverb or Adverbial Phrase to make the time or aspect of the action explicit should be continued for a long period with slow classes, because mistakes of Tense are usually very much more frequent than any other grammatical category.

It will be seen from the examples above that very little of the traditional " English Grammar," with its technical terms of Latin origin and its theoretical definitions, will be necessary during the first years of learning English; though that does not mean that no grammar—word-change, inflections, agreements, etc.—will be *learnt*. In countries where the grammar of the mother tongue has long been taught, as in France, Germany, Finland, the technical terms can be used in teaching English from the start, and parallel sentences in the mother tongue may be brought in to

---

[1] ' Aspect ' in the Verb does not tell us that an action occurs at the present time or in the future; it tells us that the action is completed, as in the Present Perfect, or is habitual, as in the Present Simple, or is continuous, as in the Continuous Present. ' Just now ' will give the ' time ' for the Present Perfect Tense.

illustrate a usage. Though even in such countries during the first few years of learning English, young pupils do not need much of this analytical grammar theory, especially as structure very often in English takes the place of inflection and word-change, as in " My uncle gave my brother a book on his birthday."

But in countries where the pupils begin to learn English before they learn the formal grammar of their mother tongue, all the commoner forms of English and all the simpler usages of Tense and Case can be taught without the use of the traditional terminology, though a few of the commonest ones may be used, as they often are used, after a year or more of oral English. For obviously, these technical terms cannot properly be understood by most of the children. If the terms are taught, these young pupils use them blindly and unintelligently. Young pupils do not need to understand much of the analytic grammar of the language they are learning: that, for instance, ' him,' ' them,' ' us ' are the Objective (or Accusative) forms of Personal Pronouns, and are used after Transitive Verbs, but that the Pronoun ' it ' has no Objective form and so can be used either as Subject or Object of a sentence. We note, too, that the time and effort expended on teaching what is a Personal Pronoun, the Objective form (or Case) of a word, a Transitive Verb, the Subject of a sentence, would have been better spent on mastering the use of those forms in sentences. For what all these younger pupils need is the frequent and meaningful use in sentences of the new inflections and forms that they are meeting for the first time, and that they require in order to make up simple sentences. Naturally, some grammar can be taught, but the description of the commoner grammatical functions is too abstract, and such intellectual studies are not fit food for the minds of the younger children.

The teaching of grammar, then, should largely be carried on through the ample use of model sentences and very numerous examples, through the use of the Direct Method, through construction exercises, such as Sentence-Completion and similar exercises, and also through intensive question and answer. The chief point to remember is that it is not the grammar of English that is so difficult: it is English usage. Therefore explanation can do little, whereas practice can do much. And any descriptions that are really necessary can usually be expressed in plain, everyday language, without making use of technical terms or difficult words; and (more important still) without bringing in any quasi-metaphysical ideas, such as " a preposition governs the Noun in the Objective Case."[1] Even such commonplace ideas as " the word qualifies the noun " cannot be truly understood by most children (or by many adults), for these so-called explanations attempt to make clear to a child relationships of meaning that have no concrete reality or interest to him.

Instead, therefore, of the traditional Grammar Lesson, in which explanation, illustration and definition loom large, the main grammar learning should be done through the pupils' using the items to be learnt. Thus the first exercises on the new grammatical form, or other item, will rely solely on imitation; the second group of exercises will require some small additions to be made to sentences by the pupils, the next group will require still more additions or changes, and the next still more. Opportunities for making mistakes in this work will be few, for the aim is to secure the frequent

[1] Prepositions in English cannot ' govern,' partly because many of them have so little meaning that they cannot affect the meaning or forms of nouns, and partly because a Preposition gets its meaning from the sentence containing it, e.g. " I write with . . .", " I cut with . . .", " I dig with . . ."; but ' come with me,' ' speak with him,' ' run with an effort.'

repetition of correct answers, so that the correct usage of the grammatical item is securely established in the pupils' speech habits. But if tricky or irregular or little understood forms and structures are given too early, mistakes are invited and often appear in quantities. The idea of this new kind of grammar teaching is not to test, and not to find out if pupils ' know ' the grammar; but to give so much practice that they will use the correct forms without fail, and often perhaps without realizing what the grammar is. For the beginners we have to establish correct language usage, not accurate grammar knowledge.

The organization of grammar exercises, especially during the first years, is so necessary and so profitable that some illustrations may help to show how simple and easily constructed exercises may be planned in a series to instil a good command of some grammatical forms. Research in the Gold Coast discovered that the expression of Number in Noun, Pronoun and Verb came second in the list of the most frequent errors during the first seven, eight and nine years of learning English. The exercises below will show some of the measures taken to remedy this weakness.

For pupils in the third, the fourth and the fifth year of learning English, Completion Exercises were recommended as part of an intensive attack on errors of Number. For instance: " Complete the following sentences: (1) The boys . . . cleaning . . . garden tools; (2) The birds . . . building . . . nests now; (3) The lorry-drivers . . . going for . . . pay to-day " (up to twenty or thirty sentences). For backward classes the Singular and Plural Verbs and Pronouns were given in brackets after each sentence, in order to reduce mistakes.

For pupils in the fourth, fifth and sixth years: " Complete the following sentences: (1) The children . . . taken . . .

toys, and . . . playing with . . .; (2) I . . . giving . . . books to my pupils for . . . to read; (3) Those boys . . . taking the books home in order to read . . . when they . . . finished . . . work."

For pupils in the sixth and seventh year: " Change the Nouns and Pronouns in the following sentences into the Plural, and the Verbs too, when necessary: (1) The house was shaken by the earthquake; (2) Before the bus was ready to go, the bus conductor was talking to his friend."

For pupils in the seventh and eighth year: " Change into the Plural only those words in the following sentences that can be used in the Plural, and where the Plural fits the sense: (1) The passenger hands his money for the fare to the bus conductor; (2) Does your sister count the change that the conductor gives her ?; (3) The bus stops at a bus-stop where a woman is standing."

Finally, we should not forget that many pupils and adults have acquired a clear enough idea of the grammatical functions of words simply by seeing them in a very large number of sentences, and not by having these functions explained to them. Grammar describes how words work together in a sentence, that is, the various ways in which they are related to each other, and the part that each plays in expressing meaning. If therefore close attention is given always to meaning, the grammatical work of most words will often be clear enough. Nevertheless, to learn a foreign language, we have to know by heart all the commoner changes in words and have a good command of their structures; if we can use these correctly we do not also have to know how to describe them. A command of structure is more easily acquired by reading, speaking and writing the language than by hearing and studying explanations.

Chapter 10

THE FIRST YEAR OF READING

In using an English Course that is planned to teach pupils primarily to read English, there is no doubt about what a teacher should do; but with a course that is mainly oral or one that is planned for more speaking than reading in the early stages, there is often confusion in the minds of teachers about how much reading should be done during the first two or three years.

We will consider a class that has had one or two years of oral English before beginning Reader One, and that reading the mother tongue has been going on for at least one year. A teacher then could spend many lessons during the first half year in teaching the children to read English. Or he could use the passages in each lesson in the Reader for material for further oral work, bringing in the reading occasionally; his plan would then emphasize the learning of spoken English, and would make use of reading as one of several methods of increasing the pupils' passive knowledge of the language. But if he wishes to teach his pupils to read English as a major accomplishment, it is essential for him to realize that courses do not always provide a training that will develop pupils' ability to read. Naturally some pupils do not need special help and training; but most of them do, especially in countries where an oral tradition is still strong, and reading is not a widespread habit.

The usual plan in oral courses in which reading is incidental is that the short passages of reading matter in each lesson provide the vocabulary, grammar, sentences and ideas for the class to work upon in order to increase their ability to use the spoken language. This is a perfectly good plan, provided the pupils are trained also to read the printed language, and are taught the various reading skills, such as reading accurately, reading aloud, reading rapidly to grasp the gist of a passage. Indeed, it will normally be most necessary for a teacher who uses such a course as we have in mind to take particular care to train his pupils throughout the first two or three years to acquire skill in exact reading. He will also have to give some careful attention to this training during the succeeding years, even though his main task is to teach the speaking of the language, because of its importance to his pupils.

After one or two years of oral work, pupils usually meet the new language in print for the first time. Some people imagine that when a class begins Reader One the teacher will have to start teaching pronunciation more seriously; but this should not be so, for by that time nearly all his pupils should have learnt to pronounce English well enough. He will, however, have to teach the letters that stand for the different sounds, and to do this gradually, beginning with sentences (well known orally by the pupils) that have no phonetic difficulties. Thus the reading of very simple English can begin before the phonetic and spelling work has progressed very far.

At the beginning of this work a teacher should read a passage to a class, at first right through slowly, and then sentence by sentence, writing on the board any symbols that the pupils have not previously met. He should avoid the use of the mother tongue, but should demonstrate meaning by action and, if simple, by explanation in English. When he is sure that the pupils understand the passage, he can set each group repeating the sentences after him in turn, reading again himself if the reading is poor. This kind of elementary reading practice might be carried on for about eight or ten lessons. The exercises and all the questions that are provided on the passage in the book should be completed, as this will clear up any difficulties and misunderstandings that were not discovered during the reading. The passage therefore will have been looked at closely, and the constant reference to the text, which is so necessary at this stage, will help the slower pupils to read. When a class has advanced far enough to be ready for more independent reading, chorus reading might be decreased. But the pace and the progress depend on the ability of the pupils, and on the thoroughness of the earlier oral work. It is impossible to plan exactly what a class should do or can do, unless it is in front of one.

This outline does not pretend to deal adequately enough with the many details of this work that should be carefully considered. The main point to keep in mind is that a class should not be rushed over the initial stage of working with a Reader. Learning to read a new language, even with a good knowledge of the meaning of the spoken language, is at first a serious difficulty for many children. Therefore the above description must be modified or changed if the method proposed does not succeed with a class. The old proverb is especially apposite here: " Make haste slowly."

We see, then, that although a course may be planned largely to teach the spoken language, yet the passages provided in each lesson for the week's oral work ought to be used always for a reading lesson as well. These passages should not be left for the pupils to look through without thorough study, or for them to read silently as preparation for speaking. They must be read carefully, some aloud, some silently; and after both readings there must be questions on the text. This is essential. The questions are to help the pupils to understand every detail in the printed word, and therefore must be very simple: for instance, the pupils read: " The woman is cooking some fufu in a big pot," and are questioned thus: " Who is cooking some fufu ? "—" What is the woman cooking ? "—" What is she doing with the fufu ? "—" What is she cooking the fufu in ? "

These " Stage One Questions " that ask only for what is in the text are asked for three purposes: one, to force the pupils to note exactly what is expressed in the printed words; two, to give them some very simple language practice; and three, to give them language practice that should always be correct—for the words and structures are right in front of the pupils' eyes. Thus, constant practice of correct sentences will establish correct language habits. We need not be continually testing the pupils: if we make them use correct sentences, then they will learn the new language correctly.

Chapter 11

LEARNING TO READ FOR EXACT INFORMATION

TEACHERS often say: "I just let the children read." But teaching children to understand the meaning of the printed words is only the beginning stage, and, though it is all important, there are other reading skills to be mastered by the children; and these skills are essential for further education. In the next five chapters, therefore, the teaching of these skills will be dealt with. It will be dealt with fully, because some aspects of reading have been lost sight of and, though some of these reading skills are the necessary equipment of all pupils who wish to enlarge their knowledge, only too often pupils leave school with no more than a basic skill of being able to read mechanically.

What we should be most concerned about is this: in teaching a second (or third) language, we do not only have to teach pupils to make out what the words mean, we should also teach them to be efficient readers of the language. To be an efficient reader, one needs to master the necessary skills. They are: the skill of reading aloud; the skill of grasping the gist of a passage; the skill of deducing information or ideas from what has been read; the skill of being able to find facts and information in books and other printed matter, and the very valuable skill of being able to note exact information when one is reading, that is, to understand exactly and fully what is in print before one's eyes.

We are dealing in this chapter with teaching this skill of acquiring exact information from books and other printed matter; and from writing. In teaching this skill, there are two slightly different objectives: one of these is the training of pupils to note exactly what is expressed, and the other is training them to find some required information or an answer to a question. The first aims at exact reading, the second at observant reading—that is quick reading when the reader is on the look-out for some fact or idea. The first is slower, careful reading, in which all the information of the page is noted and noted accurately. The second emphasizes the search for one fact or series of facts, and requires a watchfulness for what is wanted in the long stream of ideas and information that is being scrutinized in the reading. In order to find out the facts we need, we have to know where to look, and to be able to read quickly through those passages, paragraphs or pages containing information that warns us we are on the right track of what we want to know.

The methods of teaching these two related skills differ. The methods of teaching the first should be used throughout most of the course, starting quite early; for they provide excellent exercises for learning the correct usage of the new language. The teaching of the second may be left until towards the end of the course, one or two years before the boys leave school, as it is a specialized skill and can be taught to good pupils in a very short time, if they have profited from the training given to the other skills; and even slow pupils do not find it difficult.

The simplest method of increasing the exactness of reading is as follows: the pupils prepare a new passage in their Readers, reading it silently. Alternatively, though it is not so good a method, the teacher or selected pupils might read it to the class. If a passage is rather difficult, the class could work through it with the teacher, and discuss the new ideas. The second and main part of the training consists of going through the passage again, the teacher asking questions on almost every sentence. At the very beginning of this work and for some time with slow pupils, two and sometimes three questions can easily be asked on most sentences. It is important to remember always that these questions should ask only for information expressed in the sentence. These " Stage One Questions " are not intended to train pupils to think of other ideas arising out of the sentence (that is another kind of lesson). These questions have very specific purposes: they are to train the pupils to note exactly what the writer has said; and to give them practice in using the words, expressions and constructions in the passage. This practice is very simple; and it can achieve a very high degree of correctness.

At first and for a long time, the actual words and constructions of each sentence should be used in framing the questions, and nearly all of the questions can be very easy, in fact, quite obvious. But as the plan is to get correct answers each time, this simple obviousness is no disadvantage. It is quite easy as a rule to get absolute correctness in the answers, because the pupils have the passage in front of them the whole time, and can follow the text, sentence by sentence, and therefore have no trouble in seeing the correct answer.

The questions, then, ask only about the people, things, actions, referred to in the passage, and only about details actually mentioned. The questions should go from sentence to sentence in their order in the passage, so then the pupils can easily follow, and can find the answers immediately. The questioning and answering should be carried out briskly, the teacher passing from pupil to pupil without waiting if a pupil has not got his answer ready. He might sometimes ask several pupils in turn before saying which is the right one, so that more pupils have an opportunity of some language practice, and more of the class are kept busily taking part in the lesson. For the most profitable results of this work, speed is essential: it livens up language practice and ensures that all get a chance to answer.

Thus a large number of very easy questions are put to the class, and some correct language practice is rapidly obtained. Those who give wrong answers should not be corrected, but should look at the words again to find another answer. It is essential for the teacher to stick to this rule, because this work attempts to train pupils to read accurately. If he tells them the correct answer, they are not learning to read; and the ones who give incorrect answers are the very ones who need to form the habit of looking at print carefully. It is the attention of the eye to the correct forms —Tenses, Plurals, Possessives—that such questioning promotes. The speed at which it can be done, and the pupils' ambition to get a correct answer every time, make this exercise interesting to them and an effective instrument in learning.

An example of Stage One Questioning will show how easy it is to prepare, and how close to the text it should keep. Let us suppose that a class has read the following passage silently:—

"The children who live in North Africa have brown skins, brown eyes, and dark hair. For most of the year they wear thin cotton clothes because their country is hot. When they go to school they learn the same arithmetic and geography that we learn, and some of them learn English, too. . . ."

Some of the questions on this passage will be as follows:—
1. "What colour skins have children who live in North Africa?"

(The correct answer for beginners would be: "Children who live in North Africa have . . ." But more senior

pupils should say: " They have . . ."; because normal
answer forms need to be practised, as well as the full
sentence pattern.)

2. " What clothes do they wear for most of the year ? "

    (Again the beginners answer: " They wear . . ."; but
the more senior pupils reply: " Thin cotton clothes," as
this kind of reading lesson does not attempt to give
practice in using complete sentence constructions.)

3. " Why don't they wear thick clothes ? "

    (Questions asking for reasons for actions will be asked
only if the reasons are clearly expressed in the text.)

4. " What do they learn at school ? "

    (The answer, " Arithmetic, Geography and English,"
is accepted as correct; and the further question is then
asked, " Are these the same subjects as you learn ? "
Or the teacher asks: " What else does it say about these
subjects ? " Answer: " They are the same as the
subjects we learn." This probing for more complete
information is good training in efficient reading.)

With a little practice in framing questions such as these,
teachers find that they can prepare them very quickly, and
that their pupils soon become very skilful in answering them
correctly and quickly. When the children are answering
them correctly and easily, the speed of the questioning
should be increased, as that makes the children keen to take
part and to answer with enjoyment and alacrity. The next
step for them to take is for some of the class to make up
questions, and the rest of the class to answer them. Pupils
soon pick up the method of framing Stage One Questions,
and usually learn to ask them very skilfully: this gives them
further and even more intensive training in handling the
language; and they do this without the help of the teacher.
The teacher, however, often has to see that pupils' questions

are always on the text, and that they are dispersed over the class; and he will sometimes have to see that the questioning by the pupils does not drag, but that it is brisk and lively.

It can hardly be emphasized too strongly that training children like this to make up questions on the texts they are studying is language teaching of the best kind, though in very many schools it is completely neglected. It forces attention to meanings and grammatical forms and how these are used, and always with a minimum of opportunity for making mistakes; for the pupil has the text always in front of him. It is especially good language training because the pupils asking questions are using the language purposefully, because they want an answer to their question, and not because the question is " in the book " !

This kind of language practice is the most effective of all: that is, effective in producing thorough learning. The reason for this is that language that is used purposefully has behind it the strength of a human will that wants something. Thus the language makes a deeper and stronger impression on the mind of the learner than any that is given by a ' drill ' or ' completion ' or semi-mechanical exercises.

This kind of training in exact reading should go on all through the course, even though pupils become very skilful in answering correctly. Because, as the passages to be studied become longer and more informative, the pupils receive stricter training. Whenever a class learns to answer very quickly and accurately, the difficulty of the passages should be steeply increased. But normally after the first few years of this work, when the method may have been used several times a week, most pupils will not need more than perhaps one lesson a week in this Stage One Questioning. This will give more time for silent reading and for written work.

But this training in exact reading must never be disregarded or done half-heartedly, because where English is the medium of instruction, all the learning that the pupils acquire from books will depend for its value and usefulness on its accuracy, and therefore on the pupils' ability to read efficiently. We must realize, too, that every subject in the curriculum will suffer if the pupils are not trained in their English lessons to read carefully. On the other hand, if teachers in other lessons—history, geography, hygiene, etc.—in which textbooks are used freely, will question on their texts just as closely, their pupils' English will also gain from that training, and a firm foundation of knowledge of these subjects will be firmly laid.

A specimen lesson showing the actual questions and answers that occurred during Stage One Questioning is given in the Appendix; there are, however, some further points of procedure that might increase the effectiveness of the method. The amount of reading completed by a class in one lesson may often be small; but that will not matter, for the purpose of the work is to give intensive training, and not to develop ease and speed of reading. When the pupils have become skilful in giving exact answers to exact questions, then is the time to increase the length of the passages to be read silently, and the difficulty, which has already been mentioned. Then gradually the number of the questions can be reduced, and the majority of them concentrated on those parts of a chapter that need a more precise grasp of the facts or thought, or on those parts that will gain by being imagined more vividly and in greater detail. Questions for the less able pupils should be aimed at helping them to understand more clearly and imagine more precisely. But, we must emphasize, the questioning is not " to find out if the pupils have understood what they are reading." This reason for questioning is repeated over and over again, but it is not a good reason, for there is no need to find out if they understand it; it is obvious to an alert teacher if they do not (or it should be). The valid reason for questions on a text is to help the pupils, especially the slower-minded ones, to discover more in the text than they could have found out by their own efforts. And when they understand a good text fully, their enjoyment and the value of what they get out of their reading are much increased.

Stage One Questioning provides intensive training in comprehension, and is therefore a valuable part of children's linguistic education, especially if they are going to make full use of books later. It is intensive because it requires close concentration on the part of teacher and pupils. This is necessary if they are to note carefully what a writer has actually said, and if they are to understand every detail precisely. It is the kind of intensive training that is especially valuable for pupils in their second, third, fourth, and fifth year of reading English. It is not, however, the kind of questioning that is suitable for classroom work on Supplementary Readers, unless some particular passage would gain by such intensive study. Nor is it suitable for the reading lesson that aims at promoting general interest, at widening ideas, or fostering the habit of reading. Its purpose is to train pupils to get exact information from their books and other reading. Every single pupil has a right to receive this training because the possession of some precise and complete knowledge is the necessary foundation for all intellectual progress and for " The Advancement of Learning."

Reading to find required information. One of the most useful reading skills is the skill of being able to get from books the information that we need for some purpose or other. It is one that will be useful all through the lives of many of our pupils; for whenever they need the help that can be found in books, not only for instructions or advice, but also for enlightenment or entertainment, they will be able to get it quickly and easily. The acquiring of this skill, therefore, is not just another school achievement that may or may not be useful after leaving school: it is a necessity for intellectual growth and nourishment. In school, too, it is useful: there is information to be gathered from a chapter in order to write a composition, or to answer a question in geography or science; and there are facts to be collected from books on hygiene, cookery, history, botany, etc.

Pupils who have acquired this skill have a key to good work in many directions and in many walks of life. This skill, especially in understanding instructions precisely, can promote progress in almost every career, so that when we increase the efficiency of this kind of reading we are doing something especially valuable for our pupils.

But this skill is not one that most people can pick up incidentally, though some people do. Most of us need to exert a conscious effort to achieve it, and the help of a teacher. To acquire it, pupils have to read with a clear idea of what information they are looking for; it must be some detail or definite fact at first; and so they have to learn to search for the information with a question always in mind as they are reading. For instance, as they read, they might keep on asking themselves a question in order to be on the alert to find the answer. This may prevent their own personal interest and pleasure in what they are reading from holding all their attention, for they may have to read through several pages rapidly, or even a whole chapter, before the answer is complete enough. Later, they will have to learn to find the solution to a problem: this is more difficult, because they cannot be so sure what the right solution will be; and a problem for the older pupils will often be complex, and its solution may have to be collected point by point from several chapters. It would be a great advantage for the most advanced pupils if they were trained to collect information from several books.

There are several ways of planning lessons to develop this skill. At first, say for pupils in their sixth year of English or even earlier, the teacher can merely give out a question, saying: " Who can find the answer on page 30 ? " He could continue this through a short lesson, or ask questions in this way several times during other reading lessons. The first questions must require the finding of one fact only, and with a slow class this should be the rule for some time; but when the pupils discover what the procedure is, and enjoy the keen search to find answers quickly, then they may be asked questions that demand first a few, and then many details; and later, the putting together of details from several paragraphs, and then from several pages. Thus it is very easy to increase the difficulty of the tasks gradually.

Later still, the question could be written on the board, the paragraphs read silently and the answers written; in a week or so, several questions might be written on the board, and the class set to work without help or instructions from the teacher. In these lessons, when most of the pupils have found an answer, the correct version should be discussed, or the incompleteness of some of the answers might be pointed out by the pupils. Discussion will be necessary when there are alternative correct answers. Then the pupils' judgment will be brought into play in selecting the best and giving reasons for their choice.

In the following year the questions should grow more searching. It is best to have these written on the board, especially when time is needed to find the answers. These more difficult questions should require the pupils to think hard. They can be really searching because the answers do not have to be learnt or remembered, as they should be expressed in the text. Alternatively a problem could be presented: this might require information from parts of a long chapter, and of such length that the answers would have to be compiled in note form or summarized in a short paragraph. The discussion at the end would deal profitably with the relevance or necessity of those details that some of the pupils had omitted or included wrongly. If some important facts or arguments had not been found by anyone, the chapter should be read through again, with an instruction such as " There's one point that you have all missed. Try and find it." The pupils themselves should always fill in gaps left in their own work, if there is time, because the responsibility for the completeness of their work must be theirs: it is essential for their growth that they should learn to rely on themselves.

After some weeks of this work, it is a good plan to let some of the quicker ones make up questions for the class, and for them to write these on the board. Sometimes these pupils might even question the class orally, when the reading is finished. It is obvious that, if the pupils themselves have to make up the questions, their attention is drawn to the facts and information in the text, and so the efficiency of their reading is increased. It will usually be found that once the pupils discover how to frame questions on a text, they very soon learn to ask intelligent and useful ones—and sometimes very difficult ones too, occasionally even more difficult than a teacher would have asked. This is highly satisfactory because their wits are sharpened by it, and they acquire increased skill in probing the thought in the passages or books they are reading; and all this promotes full and exact comprehension.

This kind of work can be extended during the last two years of the school course, and can develop into some specially useful training for the older pupils in collecting information from books, in note-making, and in the use of dictionaries and reference books. This training is essential for those pupils whose education will continue, after they leave school, in some institution of higher studies. At first they should be set to compile notes after they have had some thorough questioning on the chapter or chapters to be studied; later, of course, this questioning would be omitted. But the prevalent practice of pupils being made to copy down summaries and notes prepared by the teacher is obviously not the best way of helping pupils to learn facts and to master a topic. It should be evident to all that most of the pupils copy down the notes from the board, or from dictation, in a mechanical way, and do not think about them or try to understand them fully, and above all they do not express the facts for themselves—and if they have not expressed these facts, they cannot be said to ' know ' them. And if they do not know them properly, how can they remember them ? They may remember the teacher's words, but this does not mean that they have acquired any knowledge.

Chapter 12

THE SKILL OF READING ALOUD

READING aloud used to be one of the normal methods for giving pupils language practice, quite regardless of its value. A lesson used to begin with pupils reading a passage aloud, usually before they knew what it was about or understood it properly. It was not realized then that if pupils did not understand fully what they were reading, they could not usually read it without stumbling or making errors of tone, emphasis or expression, quite apart from mistakes of pronunciation. Actually pronunciation mistakes were encouraged by that method, because pupils often had to pronounce words that they had never seen before. Therefore the reading aloud rarely improved, and it did not help the pupils to speak any better. Fortunately, reading aloud is not used nowadays so much, and language practice in question and answer and silent reading have a greater place in a course: the result is that there is often little time for much reading aloud. This is as it should be, for reading aloud is a special skill, and special methods are required to teach it.

Good reading aloud of a foreign language is such a special achievement that all pupils should be given special instruction, example and practice in reading their mother tongue aloud before they are called upon to read the foreign language aloud. If they learn to read their mother tongue aloud with good expression and ease, they will soon learn to read the foreign language aloud well, provided they understand fully what they are reading, and have been given special instruction and training. Unfortunately this is far from being achieved in most schools, either in the mother tongue or in foreign languages. This is partly due to the fact that teachers very often do not know exactly what this special instruction should consist of, but mostly because they will not insist on a high standard when their pupils read aloud. Far too often the reading aloud drones on without tone or stresses, so long as pronunciation is near enough to intelligibility. But if a high standard is aimed at, the pupils are aware of an objective, and this gives them some idea of what they must try to achieve, where previously they had none. Furthermore, the teacher's ambitious aim acts as a challenge to them, and inspires them to try harder—success is then possible, where formerly it was not even within sight.

The special task of teaching pupils to read a foreign language aloud should normally be carried on during the first two or three years with the Reader, and then left until the last two years of the school course. In the early years the reading aloud is useful for giving practice in pronunciation, though the amount read by each pupil should be short; for there is no point in giving pronunciation exercises unless the young reader attends closely to pronunciation. But if each has to read a long passage, attention will often be attracted to meaning, and pronunciation will be forgotten. During the last years of the course, reading aloud can be used to improve tone, rhythm and fluency; that is, as an expression exercise. At this stage a very high standard of reading should be demanded; and if this standard is not achieved, pupils should be told so: it is not good teaching, or kind, to let pupils think that their performance in speaking and reading cannot be improved.

In all this work, especially at the beginning, the main instrument that the teacher can rely on is imitation, because that is the best one to use in teaching this skill. A teacher, therefore, as has been emphasized for another purpose, is responsible for taking the greatest pains to improve his own reading aloud; to achieve perfection he will need the generous help of a very strict critic, who will listen to his reading and not let compassion allow his honesty to falter. It can hardly be denied that, as so much depends on the excellence of his own reading, all the trouble he takes to improve will not be too much.

The teacher who is to be really successful in teaching his pupils this skill must also have at his finger-tips a sound knowledge of practical phonetics, as well as the teaching skill to be able to instruct children how to correct their pronunciation and expression; he needs also the patience and unfailing care to listen acutely to his pupils' reading and to make sure they are trying to make the correct sounds. In addition, he needs skill in detecting faults and in analysing weaknesses; he is then able to give the expert advice that will help his pupils to know how to correct their faults and to improve their reading.

He must, of course, be especially careful to make sure that the passage to be read aloud is thoroughly understood; this he will do by questions that make the children think out the meaning for themselves. The more they understand of the passage by silent reading and then by thinking out answers to questions by themselves, the better they will know what to express and how to express it. By means of praise and example and expert suggestion, a teacher can inspire his pupils to put forth greater efforts and to persevere in order to try to reach a high standard; but his example must be exceptionally good, and his criticism of their reading and his suggestions will need to be well-informed, sound and able to hit the right nail on the head each time— otherwise a class *cannot* improve.

Training like this, on these or similar lines, will improve pupils' powers of comprehension, and it will help to improve their speaking. It should therefore not be neglected; for difficult as it is, a teacher should always strive to teach his pupils to speak a foreign language as if it were their mother tongue. Some teachers wisely are ambitious to strive to do this: they succeed better than those who are satisfied with reading and speaking at a lower level. The secret is " Never be completely satisfied."

Chapter 13

READING AND THINKING

THE language practice in some modern language courses is severely limited by the words and ideas in the passages provided for reading and for introducing new vocabulary, grammar, and structure. And if a teacher keeps closely to the book, his pupils will inevitably make use of the language without any active or independent mental effort. Consequently in time the resulting repetitions of language and the expression of ideas become too mechanical, especially with quick learners, or in using a course based mainly on reading. For pupils can soon acquire the skill of producing correct answers to easy questions without real thinking. Of course, the purpose of some language practice is to develop a mechanical response; but we should be on our guard to prevent reading from becoming purely automatic. To prevent this, and to ensure that the reading promotes intellectual growth, and therefore has some educative value, a second type of questioning, " Stage Two Questioning," should begin.

This kind of questioning, like that of Stage One, concentrates on the text; but it goes deeper, for it demands some thinking, and usually some imagining on the part of the pupils. This questioning, instead of asking for details given in the text, asks for further information about them. They ask, for instance: (a) what the people and things and places mentioned in the text are like; (b) why this action was done and why that one; or (c) what was the cause of this happening, and what was the result of that; or (d) how this happened, and how that. In fact, they ask for anything that can be inferred, deduced or imagined about the characters, the appearance of things or action or any other item that is mentioned in words in the passage. Thus these questions ask for anything that will serve to make the story (or whatever the passage is about) more complete, more exact, or in some way more interesting or more real to the readers, and therefore more fully understood and imagined.

As in Stage One Questioning, the pupils have their books open before them, and so can think out the answers while they concentrate on what they are reading. The idea is not to catch them, not to test them, but to help them. All that they have to do is to think more fully about the people and things mentioned in their books, and often to imagine them more vividly and realistically. For instance, one of the stories in a Reader tells us of a Tortoise that carries off a bag of salt, but no reason is given why he did so. Stage Two Questioning therefore asks: " What did the Tortoise want the bag of salt for ? " And as we do not know where he lived, why Lizard wanted the salt or what he did with it; the questions will be: " Where did Tortoise live ? "— " Why did Lizard cut the string that Tortoise had tied on to the bag ? "—" What did Lizard do with the salt ? "

This kind of questioning brings out all sorts of ideas that the children have (and sometimes curious ones), and often a lively discussion begins, and then the lesson becomes more profitable because it does not rely solely on the book, but produces fresh and varied ideas from the children, and good language practice too, because they can use the words and structures in the text, and so speak correctly. The result is that they find the stories more interesting, and they enjoy them more; thus they master the skill of following up the thought in their reading, and produce some constructive thinking.

We see, therefore, that we have not only to teach the reading of the new language; but we must also develop the ability of our pupils to think with it. Some of the teaching of reading then becomes also a training in thinking. This training will always be particularly effective because it is direct and simple, as it is based solely on the story or whatever is being read, and therefore on what is plain, straightforward and concrete; it will not be thinking in a vague, generalized, theoretical and formal way, but thinking that is factual, exact and definite.

Sometimes it is not fully recognised that the teacher of the vernacular and the teacher of foreign languages have the same valuable contribution to make to the education of children: they have the duty of training the minds of their pupils to become competent instruments for mastering the knowledge that can be obtained from books. Thus they help to make these minds capable of learning all subjects that make use of books, and capable, too, in the more active side of life, of dealing with the many and varied problems that will confront them during their whole lives. It is a great responsibility, and one that is often neglected, or but half-understood.

In addition to quickening the power of thought and imagination of children's minds, and stimulating them to a fuller response in their reading, there is another useful result of this kind of questioning. It gives rise to the expression of very simple and definite ideas. It is, therefore, a particularly good way of developing the pupils' independent use of the new language. And it is an easy way because they have a text in front of them: they can read it over silently, perhaps more than once, and can think about it before the questioning begins orally; or when they are reading if the questions are on the board. Then, as the text suggests the ideas and contains some or all of the language expressing them, very many of the answers can make use of this language; and the weaker pupils can easily answer, too. Furthermore, the pupils may prepare answers with their eyes on the book, and so achieve absolute correctness. In this way Stage Two Questioning can provide the beginnings of a freer use of the new language, and can ensure that that difficult first step to free expression and oral composition is easy, and without the usual epidemic of mistakes.

The planning of the reading programme, as we now may see, can be arranged in distinct stages, and so can ensure gradual progress in the pupils' work. First, the mechanics of reading print are mastered in the mother tongue, and then in the second language; next the skill of accurate reading is showing fruit after the first few years with the Readers; and then, as that is being improved, the reading that promotes thought and intelligent deductions is begun; this leads on to free expression, and prepares the pupils for that work. In this way the pupils' language work has continuity and a step by step advance to more valuable work.

But before leaving this topic we must look at it more widely and more deeply. First, after the early years of learning a language, this Stage Two Questioning should form part of every lesson in every subject where there is reading to be done, particularly in general subjects taught through the medium of a second language. This is important because all teachers need to be on their guard against teaching facts simply as bare facts, or in a mechanical way, without getting these facts thought about, discussed, inquired into, and if possible, used—for provoking further ideas, for drawing deductions, for relating to other similar contexts and fields of study or experience.

In lessons on other subjects, therefore, where much new information is to be learnt, it is not at all satisfactory for a teacher to rattle off all that he has prepared, and then to question the class on what he has said, in order to find out if the pupils know it—that kind of knowing is mere verbal acquaintance and verbal acceptance without any firm roots of understanding and conviction. Much more is needed for acquiring the true knowledge that is characterized by a hard grasp of concrete fact and tinctured with insight and imagination: that is real knowledge. So all explanation and description should be interspersed throughout with questions, stimulating the pupils to think about what is said, and inciting their minds to probe deeper. For, if everything is told to a class straight off, that will not help the pupils to find interest in the subject, or to understand it thoroughly—or to remember it. Therefore, if a topic has any value, it must be worked into the pupils' thinking about it and into their previous knowledge of it and of related topics that they already have studied. It must be turned over in their minds before it slips away like quicksilver in the palm of your hand. It must be applied, either intellectually or physically, but preferably both. It needs to be examined, seen in action, discussed, meditated upon; in fact, it has to be incubated in the warm inspiration of their enquiring minds. Then, it will enrich those minds, and perhaps bear fruit in their lives.

So we see that Stage Two Questions require the pupils to take a small step forward in thought, training them to think precisely about facts and real things, and which is still more important perhaps, to think independently. In this way a pupil learns to rely on his own powers, and he sees that he is adding to his store of idea and knowledge. This encourages him to continue to build up ideas concerning all that he reads about; and these engage his interest more deeply

E

still. His accumulation of simple and concrete ideas and his growing interest in them are the basis that he needs for constructive thinking. Thus he is trained to use his mind efficiently and profitably; he learns to look more deeply into causes and results, into motives and reasons, and he learns how to draw sound conclusions and inferences from all that he hears and sees and reads. And he begins to read more widely in the foreign language—his world can never be too large for him; and so all his reading becomes of value to him, stimulating and storing his mind; and his efficiency and skill in reading and thinking make the knowledge he has obtained available for further progress.

Chapter 14

THE SKILL OF EFFICIENT SILENT READING

WE come now to a much neglected aspect of reading. Being able to read rapidly to oneself is an essential skill for all students: it enables them to enlarge their knowledge, to find recreation and enjoyment, and to improve their technical achievements in many different ways. It is a skill that pupils in school and young students embarking on further education need for their studies. They need skill in rapid silent reading (*a*) in order to be able to seize the gist of a passage in the books they have to study; (*b*) in order to be able to find out what some expert has said on some subject; and (*c*) in order to be able to read quickly through books which will not repay careful study, yet which will enlarge one's ideas or in some other way are worth attention.

In countries where pupils read widely in the mother tongue, this skill in reading books in a foreign language will not be such a very valuable acquisition. But in countries where most or all of the wider reading in many subjects has to be done in a foreign language, as must be necessary in many parts of Africa and elsewhere, the acquiring of this skill is essential.

In addition to this, rapid reading should be carried out by all students of foreign languages in order to increase their vocabulary and the ease and fluency of their reading; and also in order to maintain their command of the language during periods of absence, illness and after leaving school. Wide and regular reading consolidates all that has been gained, and accustoms the mind to make use of a language as a natural and familiar medium of thought and communication.

We are concerned here mainly with improving ease and fluency of silent reading; not with precise comprehension of sentence and idea. This kind of reading is not intended to lead to the active use of new words or the learning of new expressions; but to improve recognition and response to the words and constructions already learnt, and especially to make recognition immediate, and response quick.

Looking back, we see that the learning of new items of language needs close intensive work, drill and controlled usage. Then comes extensive and uninterrupted reading of much easy and interesting matter in order to improve the learner's ease and familiarity with those items and with all that has already been learnt. Both types of work are necessary: intensive study and usage, and extensive reading for practice in quick and easy recognition.

There is a further reason for encouraging rapid silent reading: we want our pupils to acquire the habit of reading, so that they will continue to learn and to gain knowledge, and especially to profit from all that a literature of the new language offers them. If they can read with ease, and do not have to plough through books slowly, they will enjoy them more, and are much more likely to read them. If they can read rapidly, they can read more, and can find out before they leave school what books there are for them to enjoy and make use of; they also find out where they can turn to for information, and for their spiritual and intellectual needs.

There are two language learning abilities that rapid silent reading especially fosters: the learning of new words and the quick grasp of meaning. Wide easy reading is essential for all language learners because numbers of new words are added to one's passive vocabulary, and because the ability to deduce the meaning of unknown words from their contexts is brought into play, and thereby sharpened. This linguistic ability is a most valuable one for all those who will continue to learn and read languages. Unfortunately, language teachers do not always know that this ability comes into action whenever a learner is reading a text containing unknown or imperfectly known words, and so they tell pupils these meanings, and thus prevent the ability from developing, or they encourage the immediate use of the dictionary, instead of first asking a question that will help the pupil to infer the meaning of the word from the sense of the words accompanying it.

As for the enlargement of the passive vocabulary, this can occur for most students only through rapid silent reading, unless the learner is often in the company of those who use the foreign language freely in conversation. So this kind of reading is especially important for those who are likely to make extensive use of the language, and who wish to master it completely—and retain their command of it.

In order to develop the skill of rapid silent reading one thing is essential in the early stages: the passages selected must be easy. The texts for slow readers should at first be those that had been prescribed for a lower class. If many of the class have read a text previously, this will ensure that the reading is really rapid. But whenever possible, fresh and unseen texts should be chosen. For when slow pupils find that they can read unseen passages easily, they gain confidence in their own abilities. It is always very helpful for backward pupils to find that they do not always need a teacher's intervention: this often unnoticed impulse stirs them to make an effort.

It is a good plan with slow classes to set at first a limited amount to be read in a limited time, even as little as a page or only a few paragraphs. After the reading, a few questions are asked on the general content of the passage, and then the silent reading starts again, this time on a somewhat longer passage; then more questions at the end; and then more reading on a still longer piece; thus a long chapter is broken up. This helps the slower and less intelligent pupils to keep their minds on the reading, for they have not a long task beyond their powers, and it spurs on the very slow readers, so they do not lose heart by being left far behind at the end of a long silent reading period. The questions here, we may remind ourselves, are merely to ensure that the passages are not read too carelessly; they are not a detailed test of understanding. The aim is to obtain a general understanding of the passage quickly.

If after three or four questions, the answers show that parts of the passage have not been fully understood, a class should be set to read it again, especially a very lively class, and then questioned again. Usually it will be found that a second reading and questioning help the pupils to understand difficult passages in the chapter; but often misunderstandings are due to careless reading. If there are frequent misunderstandings, then perhaps the chapter is too difficult for the class, or for this kind of independent reading. Explanations of points which might baffle the children should be given only on rare occasions, as self-reliance in using books is so important for the more able pupils. Normally, therefore, as soon as three or four questions have been answered reasonably well, the class should read on, even to the end of a long chapter, while their interest is still alive.

Some written work, even a few lines, in a reading lesson is a wholesome check on the pupils who are doing all the answering; and those who avoid effort must be stirred up to take part in the work. Furthermore, to have some written

answers at the end of a silent reading lesson helps to con-
solidate the ground by getting individual expression of what
has been read, and gives language practice to the slower ones.

We should not forget that questions in most kinds of oral
work should usually be given to the whole class, without an
individual being named, so that all may get an answer ready
before the one to answer is indicated. On occasions like
this, and when questions are written on the board to be
answered orally, a high standard of correctness can be
demanded in the answers, because all have had time to
prepare correct answers. Questions after silent reading can,
however, be more difficult, and should demand more
thought, than those fired rapidly at a class in the intensive
study of a text.

Finally, we might look again at the importance of this
topic: the developing of skill and interest in silent reading.
There is a very great need for all those who are going on to
higher education to be able to find facts and information
quickly from books; for there is far too much to learn for
them to spend long hours over every book that they have
to read, estimable and necessary at times as conscientious
study is. Facility in reading must be acquired as well as
thoroughness, each in its place. And if the best pupils are
to acquire scholarly habits, they must be able to verify their
facts and references without holding up their closer and
wider reading, and such verifications eat up time; but the
ability to go quickly through a book will help considerably.

Almost every student who is going to specialize should
try to acquire this skill of rapid reading, for there is a special
need then to read widely in and outside a subject, if a student
is to become knowledgeable, broad-minded and truly master
of his subject. But all pupils at school should also read
widely, while they have the opportunity, in order to acquire

some breadth of mind in human affairs. They should read easy and interesting books, plays, travels, history, biography, adventure, scientific discoveries and achievements, and pioneering expeditions in the less accessible parts of the world, and also not only the easier novels of a few well-known novelists, but some of the finest works of the great writers.

Chapter 15

WIDE READING AND ITS VALUE

THE value of being able to read easily and of acquiring the habit of reading is undeniable: the pupil meets with new ideas, and his mind assimilates many of these without laborious effort; he acquires a broadening fund of fact and information about a variety of subjects; he learns about the lives of other people and about life in other lands, and so his sympathetic understanding of others is nurtured; he enriches his mind and imagination with new and significant ideas and experiences, and so he becomes not only a useful citizen of his own country, but a worthy and respected " Citizen of the World."

But what is more immediately relevant to the average pupil in school is that he will be able to make good progress in almost any subject that he has the ability and the opportunity to study, if he has acquired the habit of reading. And the pupil who will eventually make some contribution, even if a small one, to the welfare, government or social life of his countrymen, will make a better one undoubtedly if he is a wide reader. Therefore, if a teacher trains his pupils to master this skill, he is equipping them with a master-key that will open many doors that lead to the road of learning and enlightenment.

But in order to develop this skill and this habit, one ingredient is all important: interest. Where there is interest, there can be speed, accuracy and improvement in reading efficiency; without it, all will suffer. Indeed, without interest, success perhaps is unobtainable. Interest is all-important because understanding and imagining are more active where there is true interest. In fact, they become fully active only when interest is aroused; then they play a stronger and more vital part in the process of learning, establishing the foundations, relating fact to reality, retaining what has been gained, and stimulating progress.

To get the best out of a book, such as a good novel, the reader needs at first to become so absorbed in the story that he is carried along by the rapid action and feels himself to be taking part in the adventure, enjoying the quick succession of dangers and hardships that the hero goes through—and finally escapes from. The frequent absorption of a young reader in exciting stories in this way trains him to read fluently and accurately, for his mind is glued to the page and he wants to know everything that happens. And with every book he reads and enjoys, the habit of reading becomes more firmly established—and all the time he is becoming more and more at home with the foreign language.

The very useful part, then, that a teacher can play in this is to help his pupils to find interest in the stories they have to read and to become absorbed in them. He can recommend books to individual pupils, discovering those that are likely to be suitable to their tastes through a close and sympathetic understanding of their likes and dislikes, and of their abilities.

If school-children are to master a foreign language and to be able to make good use of it after their school days, they must read a great deal, for that is one of the best ways of learning to think in the new language. For many of us it is the only way of achieving a mastery of a new language, and of being able to appreciate its peculiar quality and nature, as we may not have the opportunity ever of putting the final polish on it during a visit to the foreign country. Therefore every teacher of foreign languages ought to devote special thought and effort to the promotion of their pupils' interest in wide reading; and it would be most advisable for him to allot time during the course to the fostering of this habit, especially in the upper classes of the school.

Clearly it is not enough merely to insist that pupils should read widely, and that they should buy books for this purpose. Special methods have to be devised to help pupils to improve in fluency of reading, for that will stimulate interest. The ordinary lesson will do little, if anything, to inculcate this habit; and too much reading aloud will hinder it, for listening to poor readers stumbling through a good story does not increase the listeners' interest or their absorption in it.

It is not always a difficult task to develop pupils' interest in wide reading: a variety of ways of attacking the problem and the patience and enthusiasm to keep up an unflagging campaign are usually enough to bring some success. Let us run through some of the ways of promoting interest in reading. Enjoyable stories from Supplementary Readers (or parts of them) and from other books can be used for some of the oral work, and for free compositions in the middle and upper classes; for instance, by re-telling a story to a class, or having a story re-told as if by an eye-witness, or as if one of the characters had told it. Sometimes a likely book can be introduced to a class by selecting from it some exciting passages for intensive questioning, either Stage One or Stage Two Questioning, especially asking questions that might help to make the scene more vivid or realistic. Subjects of interest can be taken from these stories for discussion in the oral course; pupils can question a whole class briefly on the stories they have read; and perhaps even, pupils could question each other quietly; though this is not to be recommended for every school, as it calls for exceptional qualities in a teacher, and sometimes in the school as well;

nevertheless, some teachers have been able to use this method with success. Its unsuitability for some classes should not blind us to its soundness and fruitfulness.

Then, every teacher should occasionally read aloud to his class, setting himself out to try to help his pupils to enjoy passages of special interest or excitement; though he would have to be careful not to make the reading too emphatic or too dramatic in his enthusiasm to achieve his object. He should usually choose passages for this purpose which he himself has liked, or which excite curiosity and conjecture. He might do this reading in a special " Story-Telling " period at the end of the week; and could vary it by letting each pupil tell a part of a story to the class, or he could read aloud one or two short passages from it, simply to stimulate interest. In the middle and senior classes pupils could be encouraged to talk about whatever has interested them in their Readers and in their wider reading. The class then could discuss these topics, supporting their opinions by reference to details in their books. Or they could discuss which is the most exciting incident in a story, which character they liked best and why, which were the saddest or the most humorous parts, and other similar topics arising from their reading—almost anything will serve, provided further interest in reading is aroused.

One of the best ways of increasing interest and enjoyment in a story is to have parts of it acted in class, either extempore while someone is reading the passage aloud or worked up more carefully into a short scene or two-scene play by the children, as part of their written work, and then acted. In doing this, action and simple dialogue should be discussed and tried over, and then written out fully, corrected and perhaps added to and altered until quite suitable for acting; thus a simple play for classroom use is produced.

By having two or three groups as separate acting companies most of the class can be given some part in the speaking, in the preparation or in the production. But the aim of this work should not be forgotten : it is to foster and increase interest in the characters and the story. There should therefore be no thought of producing the play as entertainment, though it might grow into that, and no thought of training pupils to act; so if it is done crudely, that will not matter, provided the actors are intent on it.

Of course, much can be done to stimulate wide reading through the School Library, or by working up a small Form Library. For instance, by having " Library Periods," when a class is taken to the library, books can be discussed and sampled and become known. Or the period may be used for collecting information for work in other subjects, for general interest, or for English Compositions. By having " Library Readings " for half-an-hour before an afternoon session twice a week, by issuing a book-list to each pupil of books he ought to read, and by other ways of introducing books to the class, a general keenness for reading can gradually be developed through the school, especially if several of the staff join in the drive for more reading, and if the Headmaster backs the scheme with his active co-operation.

Something, too, can often be done by gentle pressure and persuasion to urge pupils in the upper classes to buy a few books, and to make full use of the Public Library, where there is one, if it is not already popular, as usually it would be. But help in the library itself is needed by many pupils: they have to learn where to look, how to use a catalogue and even the kind of book they should take out. Here the teacher's regular presence is always a great help, especially where the Library staff have not organized a " Children's

Corner." Even those schools far from big towns and Public Libraries, can now, in most countries, usually have boxes of books sent to them every month. Librarians in Public Libraries are nearly always very willing to help, and will do a great deal for a school that is determined to do all that is possible for their pupils' reading. Teachers should visit the local libraries and find out what is possible. If library and school staffs can meet and discuss pupils' needs and a plan of action, that would be no doubt most profitable.

One last point: many people think that reading matter for wide reading in a foreign language must be of good quality. This is a mistake. It is certainly necessary to have a high standard in most aspects of language learning, as has been pointed out, but it is not necessary in this one. As long as the writer's use of words is reasonably good, and the structure of his sentences normal, it does not matter if the material for wide reading is not " good literature." Even the paraphrased and simplified versions of classical novels will serve well enough at first; but always the shortened, unparaphrased versions will be better for this purpose than the simplified series. Indeed, these shortened editions will be better even than the complete long novels of Scott, Dickens, Thackeray, for the less expert readers get tired of very long stories, and will not persist long enough for good reading habits to form. It would be better to use short stories, folk-tales and fables and adventure stories at first.

Chapter 16

ORAL COMPOSITION

WE are dealing here with the spoken English that consists of more than a simple answer to a question, more than a single sentence—Simple, Compound or Complex, and more than a short remark or comment in discussion. Therefore we do not include here those oral exercises in which pupils make up sentences or complete them. Such exercises, used frequently during the first three years, will be preliminary preparation for oral composition. They will, however, be useful throughout an English course as ' drill ' exercises, whenever new grammatical forms and structures are introduced, or later when these need renewed practice. In this chapter we are to consider short explanations, descriptions, short stories, accounts of local events, short speeches, somewhat formal discussion and all oral work of that kind. We must first, however, consider the purpose of oral composition, and its value in learning a language, as well as in educating our pupils.

Oral composition is especially useful for giving practice in using the language already learnt so that pupils begin to feel thoroughly at home with it, and to use it so confidently that it does not impede the efficiency of their thinking. It is extremely important for pupils in many countries that their use of English shall be established and consolidated in their linguistic habits as a natural reaction in conversation, business discussions and in all other occasions for speech in the foreign language.

Oral composition is also useful for training pupils to express their interests, feelings, ideas, needs and knowledge in the new language, and to express these as clearly and correctly as they would in their own mother tongue. We should expect our pupils to be able to make competent use of the new language, speaking freely and correctly to friends, acquaintances and strangers, among relatives and neighbours in social gatherings, and in home life, where the language is welcomed. To achieve competence such as this, most pupils need long and careful teaching, which should make use of oral composition as the main method.

As regards language learning, the value of good oral composition is that it teaches good spoken English. There is no need to dwell on this in countries where there is a long and fine oral tradition; though where schooling is thought of mainly as book learning, the need for good speaking is often overlooked. Among most educationists nowadays the value of clear and intelligible speech is widely recognized. Good oral work has a special value in education: it trains pupils to think clearly and precisely, for muddled thoughts often become clarified when they are given oral expression. To speak to an audience, if only a classroom one, forces a speaker to express his thoughts more intelligibly and correctly than he would when thinking them over to himself. For thoughts, whether spoken aloud or expressed in writing, have to be framed in one of the accepted sentence-patterns of the language, and with some degree of grammatical correctness, otherwise they would be un-intelligible or confusing. It is the knowledge that someone is listening (or will read) that forces a speaker to make himself understood; and this continual striving to make himself understood will gradually help a speaker to improve his ability to communicate what is in his mind. We have all felt the necessity to make ourselves understood by an audience—in the classroom, in a pulpit, in a political meeting or a debating society—and it is this feeling that trains a speaker, forcing him to use language better than his inner customary thinking requires. By dint of speaking to an audience, even if to an audience of only one, we can improve our speaking of a foreign language; but we do need the audience, and our pupils and the classroom oral composition lesson provide this.

When we think of all the oral work that the pupils have done in the classroom, and when we recall how many mechanical repetitions are needed, we realize how rarely any pupil has felt any real necessity to make himself understood during the first years of learning a new language. We then perceive how feeble and artificial the stimulus is that a pupil usually receives to improve his command of language. He repeats the sentence that he hears, he completes sentences that are in the book, he constructs a sentence on the pattern of a given one; but he rarely expresses what he is thinking, for most of the time he is thinking what the book requires him to think. These mechanical drill sentences are of course necessary; but an undiluted diet of them is not. And when they go on year after year without sufficient story-telling and dramatic work or any other real language practice, they are deadening. There must be occasions when the pupils feel the necessity to inform someone of something, to explain, to instruct, to entertain with a story, so that the language then has behind it the force of a speaker's purpose and intention. Oral composition will provide this.

There is another point of wide importance in education: good oral composition promotes the clearer and more precise thinking that will help to make the learning of all the other subjects on the curriculum more exact, and therefore more perfectly understood and remembered. Then if these other subjects that involve the use of language are also taught with a strict regard for exactness of language, the facts and ideas to be learnt by the pupils will be understood with more exactness, and therefore will be remembered better. The pupils will also be able to express what they have learnt with greater exactness: thus further advance in the subject is possible.

Very simple language does not necessarily favour sound learning in all subjects: clear and exact language is required, even if it is not simple. It is a fatal error to simplify the language so competently that the mind of the learner has only vague ideas and watered-down facts to grasp. If that is done, the intellect has nothing sharp in outline to grip on to, but only ideas without ' form.' And if the pupil has only vague ideas about history, geography, science, etc., he cannot understand these subjects properly, and he cannot make sound progress, or indeed any progress. If, however, a pupil can write down the knowledge that he has on some subject in precise terms, then we may be assured that he not only knows it, but knows that he knows it—and *that* gives him confidence and satisfaction in learning. Therefore he takes another step forward, and in this way gradually masters the facts and ideas of the subject he is studying. In our thinking and planning for education, we must be on our guard against the errors of diluting thought by simplifying the language so much that there is nothing left to understand, and of under-estimating the need for fostering pupils' confidence in their ability to master definite knowledge.

To help a class to produce good oral composition is not easy; but the secret of it is always to have some preparation beforehand, and to see that this preparation is thorough. It is essential to have especially careful preparation for pupils who find difficulty in speaking, or who quickly run out of ideas, or who hesitate frequently or become tongue-tied. This preparation needs to be continued until these pupils can stand up and speak continuously for two or three minutes—and that is quite a long time for a slow pupil. The preparation should continue as long as this because, if a pupil has to stand up and try to think of something to say, and is not able to do so, or if he comes to a full stop after a sentence or two, his ability to make progress in this work suffers a setback. Children must not be allowed to get into difficulties like this, because their self-confidence becomes undermined, and they are unable to think or speak. Thus the skill that the teacher hopes to develop does not even become active. Only too often that very element that will ensure progress—self-confidence—is destroyed during the lesson where it is needed most. Indeed, self-confidence is a much more precious possession than most of us realize.

Preparation for oral composition at first has to be quite simple. The class that is ready to begin such work need not have an outstandingly good command of English, because only subjects that have been dealt with fully in reading and written work should be used at first for oral composition. So the subject should be well known to the class and the vocabulary familiar. For this work is not intended to enlarge vocabulary or to practise the expression of difficult ideas and thought. Its purpose is to increase the fluent use of English, and to give ease and confidence in speaking. A class that has had good oral exercises and plenty of oral questioning, should be ready for this work perhaps by the middle of their fourth or fifth year of English, if they have begun learning it before the age of eight or nine. But those beginning English in their secondary school should perhaps be given some simple oral composition in their third year, if not before. It is not possible to suggest the best time to begin, because classes differ so much, and some teachers have special aptitudes for bringing on pupils in free, everyday speech in a new language.

At first there cannot be much variety in the preparation for oral composition. It is sometimes advisable not to emphasize that much more difficult work is to be attempted; but to make a smooth transition to it from the accustomed types of oral exercise that the class has been doing. It is easy to increase the oral questioning on some familiar topic so that the expression of what is known about it may be fully revised and corrected. Then by demanding longer answers very gradually, the pupils learn to make quite well-connected statements about the subject; for instance, about their games, their homes, relatives, visits, or whatever has been chosen because it is known from first-hand experience, and is of sufficient interest to the children. Thus a class can be led into the new type of work, instead of being abruptly confronted by a strange task, and so feeling hesitant or doubtful about being able to do it. This applies only to younger or backward pupils, for the challenge of a new task will be stimulating to intelligent and to older pupils.

The Reader that a class has been using will provide much material for oral composition. At first the younger ones can reproduce whole paragraphs orally from their books, either keeping close to the text, or making use of forms of expression they have learnt. The weaker pupils at first should reproduce only those paragraphs that they have recently studied; and these might be read through again silently at the beginning of the lesson. The principle is that the more thorough the preparation, the better the oral will be, and for these weaker pupils the preparation can hardly be too thorough. When they have found that they can reproduce whole paragraphs orally without looking at the book, they will be ready to attempt something slightly more difficult. Again, it is easy to lead them on, by asking questions, to express other ideas on the same subject than those in the text, and then from well-known passages to express similar ideas and experiences in paragraphs of their own. This kind of guidance in step by step progress is possible because the gradual increase in the demands of the questions can be controlled, and can be suited to the interests and abilities of the class. The teacher can soon see if the questions are demanding too much, or on the other hand, if they do not stimulate the pupils to talk freely about what they know.

The best kind of preparation for the younger pupils is supplied in story-telling. First, stories from their Readers and then fresh ones are told by the teacher, and then the children should reproduce those that they have heard at home; though the quicker ones may not need that stage. Simple questioning will refresh their memories, and will give them a little practice before the full story is told. The weaker the pupils are in using the language, the more questioning there must be, for that will reduce mistakes and help to produce connected narrative. In telling a story for the first time, each pupil should contribute a small section; and after that the complete story can be told by a few pupils re-telling longer sections. In the next stage pupils prepare short stories and anecdotes that they have found in magazines and library books; but it is always better to start with those that they have heard in their villages and at home, for they know these, and such stories will be more suited to their interests.

Usually it is better to plan the story-telling in small groups, if the class has been trained to work like that, so the supply of stories will be sufficient perhaps for several lessons. Folk tales and fables of their own people, which the children are accustomed to hear in their mother tongue, will be especially suitable for re-telling in English, if the pupils are advanced enough to manage the simple translations. If these tales are very simple, as many of them are, and very well known, they may be used in the English lesson at an early stage.

Whenever less well-known subjects are proposed by the older pupils, there must be especially thorough questioning in order to help these pupils to perceive their ideas more clearly, to learn to express unfamiliar facts and to understand the subject more fully. It is best at first, and with weak classes for a long time, to write up all suggestions on the board, so that these will remind speakers what to say. The pupils can look at the notes on the board as they speak, if necessary; and as they wait for their turn, the suggestions on the board may remind the quicker ones of other things to say. If there are many suggestions, they might be grouped on the board, and then different pupils or groups of pupils could speak on different aspects of the subject, though this kind of work is better for later on in the year.

When improvement in speaking has been achieved, only the key words and phrases referring to the points suggested by the class should be written on the board, and this kind of guidance continued for a term or more. Later, the notes and key words may be written up, discussed, perhaps added to, and then rubbed out before the speaking begins. In the last stage, when the pupils have shown real aptitude in speaking, the questioning is carried out as before, but the pupils make their own notes on paper, and silently prepare their speeches. At first they may refer to their notes, but later they should try to speak without looking at them. It will be necessary for a teacher always to make sure that the notes of the weaker pupils are much more detailed than those of good speakers, and at first that they are written out in full, and possibly revised by him. The first speeches of the pupils of poorest ability should no doubt be learnt by heart. Later, these pupils should learn their notes by heart, for a setback at first may well hinder progress later.

Later still, when the pupils have learnt to make notes and to use them while speaking, they can prepare stories, arguments, explanations, addresses for public ceremonies, etc. The information and ideas might be collected from books or other sources, and summarized in note form before the lesson. Less able speakers might learn by heart the opening sentences of their talk, and many of them will still need help in making notes, in spacing these out to make them easy to read, and in short sentences or headings, for these notes must be in a form that can be used by a less able mind and a less observant intelligence.

It is best to choose simple and matter-of-fact subjects for the argument or discussion type of talk, such as " Is one type of game better than another ? "; " Shall we choose this play or that for a performance at the end-of-term concert ? " Pupils often have to be encouraged to produce reasons for their proposals, as they do not always realize that these are necessary. At this stage, when few pupils can use the language well enough for debating, they can easily prepare five or six reasons for their plan or proposal; and that will be good training for the debate later, a training that is nearly always needed. If a class is sitting in pairs or fours, one of each pair can prepare reasons for a proposal, and the other his reasons for opposing it: they then weigh up the reasons and try to estimate who has the stronger case. This might be carried on for some weeks until the class is well prepared for informal debating. Planning a method on wide lines and arranging the work to proceed step by step like this is more necessary for the success of formal debating than for almost any other part of the language course.

After about four or five years of English, pupils should be ready for speaking on subjects that lend themselves naturally to discussion. It is easy to start this off during the questioning by asking: " Do you all agree with that ? " or " What are the arguments against that ? " When other points of view have been expressed, and reasons for these demanded, a discussion will often develop without further impetus from the teacher. This kind of work, where pupils are arguing with one another, is valuable training, because then they are using English to express their own ideas and perhaps beliefs that they hold rather strongly. They are, therefore, using the language purposefully, and this helps their command of it to become more natural and fluent. Of course, their strong feelings may lead them to exaggerate, or to be inaccurate, or to bring in arguments that are illogical or even completely irrelevant. These might be common faults, so a discussion often has to be controlled with a firm but unobtrusive hand.

Chapter 17

STEPS TO 'FREE' WRITTEN WORK

WRITING a foreign language is a stern check on incorrectness, and therefore should be demanded by all teachers, even if his pupils may never need to write the language. Unfortunately many pupils make slow progress in this work, and so their language learning is held up. It is necessary, therefore, to find out why one's pupils are making little progress. There are normally four main causes for a lack of progress in writing a foreign language: inadequate preparation for the writing; having to write without purpose or objective; lack of help that shows exactly how to improve the writing; unsuitable subjects to write about. Let us consider the first problem, that of adequate preparation.

Until pupils are at the top of a secondary school it is essential for them to have thorough preparation for all written composition work. This preparation should nearly always be carried out orally, except late in the course when it can be done from books independently. For without careful preparation, writing compositions will not help much in the learning of a new language. If pupils have to rack their brains for something to say, or if they try to express something beyond their powers, the writing may be more harmful than helpful. That is not the way to acquire facility and correctness in language. We have to be wary, too, of providing easy opportunities for mistakes. From every point of view good preparation is valuable: it can enlarge vocabulary, improve choice of words, and establish correct usages. It can teach an orderly arrangement of facts, and can increase fluency and clarity. As with oral composition, the better the preparation, the better the written work.

Some of the well-proved types of preparation for pupils who have learnt English for about six or seven years are:—

(i) **Oral Questioning.** This should usually be energetic and detailed. It should be well distributed over the class. But it must be focused on definite aspects of the subject, so that every question will impel the pupils to think more precisely about details. It should drive the pupils to discover more and more details, and to think precisely of facts, ideas, and of everything related to the subject. There is no profit in stimulating pupils to produce generalizations and obvious platitudes. It should be the teacher's aim to have his pupils' minds seething with ideas; for it would be useless to try to give practice in using a language if the pupils had little to express, or if all that they had to say were vague, general or imperfectly known. The object of this preparation is to give the pupils practice in presenting facts and ideas in the new language; therefore it is important, and must not be slipshod: if it is, it will defeat the object of the composition.

(ii) **The Use of Pictures.** To have pictures or one large picture providing information for written work can always be a help if proper use is made of it. This type of preparation is especially useful at the beginning of a course of writing, especially at the end of the ' bridge ' period that leads from exercises to the writing of short paragraphs. The main part that the teacher plays is to be the questioner, as before. He has to draw the pupils' attention to things in the picture about which there is something to say; though at first questions are always necessary in order to help pupils to see what is in the picture and to note exactly what is there for them to think about. Therefore the questions should first ask about the subject of the picture, what people and things are to be seen, and what these are doing. These first questions should be very easy and should ask for what, to us, is obvious.

It is necessary to emphasize this, for pupils do not see what we see, and those who need this help are often weak or careless observers: they see only the general subject or merely a few details in the picture, or they are lazy-minded and are not accustomed to give more than cursory attention to a picture. So, we repeat, the questions ask at first just what can be seen; but every detail possible must also be found and expressed by the pupils. They must not be told anything.

When the picture has been well studied, questions to stimulate the pupils' imaginations will be asked; for instance, what the people in the picture might have been doing earlier, what they might do next or later on, what kind of people they are, and why they are doing the actions we have noted ? With good classes, simple stories of incidents in these people's lives will be thought of, and short narratives begin to emerge. This may not happen at first; if it does not, a teacher should not try to force the pace in order to get narratives going; but if his questions are detailed and are focused on human beings and their doings, then narrative will often begin naturally. This leads on later to more complete story-telling, and " Picture Compositions " can be fruitful preparation and training for this work.

During this early stage, it is necessary to write on the board all the new words, phrases and sometimes whole sentences that have been suggested as the result of questions. Those that have an unusual structure, or that are useful for stimulating further thought, might be left on the board throughout the lesson and perhaps copied into exercise books. As for the Oral Composition, so here, words and notes should be left on the board at first for the writers to use if they need them; and this procedure should be continued for as long as the class need such reminders. With backward classes most of the words that are habitually mis-spelt or wrongly inflected will have to be written on the board. It is best for the pupils themselves to do this, as these pupils should have all the easy practice possible in writing the new language correctly.

The pictures in most of the published English Courses are too simplified for effective use in Picture Compositions; many teachers therefore make it a practice to collect all the pictures they can lay their hands on, and soon have a full file of postcards, snapshots, photographs cut from periodicals, advertisements, etc. The small pictures are suitable for the more senior classes, when each pupil or pair can have one, so that variety and individual interests can be fostered; but for the younger ones the larger pictures of the pictorial magazines are the best.

(iii) **Reading Aloud.** The reading aloud by teacher of an extract or two from interesting articles, magazines, reference books, etc., will provide fresh and varied preparation for writing. After the reading there should nearly always be some oral questioning, especially with poor classes. These questions should be on the content, its usefulness, its application or relevance to other subjects; they should stimulate further thought; and if the class is very intelligent, they should enquire deeply into the subject, or widely into related subjects. We should not forget that the mistake of not making questions difficult enough for good classes often produces boredom, half-hearted effort and laziness.

Later on, pupils should read the extracts aloud to the class, even selecting the material themselves if they have the books or can get them from the library; they might even read several extracts from different books, for that would stimulate thought. No opportunity of handing over small responsibilities like these to the pupils, especially to the restless and inattentive ones, should be missed.

(iv) **Short Speeches and Lectures.** Short addresses or informal talks may be used towards the end of the course as preparation for written work. They have to be carefully prepared, if possible in small groups. At first they should be read to a class by the group leader. After the reading, the pupils question the reader in order to understand the facts and ideas more clearly and fully. This questioning should always be encouraged, as it makes the writer think harder and more precisely, and it helps poorer pupils to remember what they have forgotten to put in.

(v) **Silent Reading.** The best kind of preparation for the older pupils is the reading silently of textbooks, Supplementary Readers, library books and magazines in class. With all but the best classes there should be some oral discussion before writing, so that the weaker ones will be helped. If there is no discussion after reading, the class might discuss and plan what they will look for in their preparatory silent reading, as this sometimes is helpful.

Older pupils could be encouraged to find sources of information themselves, and to bring material to school for study and the collecting of facts. Sometimes it is possible for a class to borrow books from the school library, returning them at the end of the double period that would be necessary for work like this. The pupils would then have some training in the use of the library, a training that most of them need; it also trains them to make use of books, another necessary accomplishment for students. But, unfortunately, often school libraries are allowed to become derelict, thus revealing a woeful neglect of opportunity by the teachers of

English, who could do so much through the library to help the pupils' learning of English; perhaps they do not see that it is better to wear out the books by constant use than to leave them on the shelves to be eaten by insects and rotted by the damp.

(vi) **Out-of-School Preparation.** Instead of having all preparation for writing done in school, it is often better to encourage the senior pupils to ' get up ' a subject out of school. Pupils can often do this, sometimes by reading up the subject in the school or public library, or by asking relatives and friends about it. But the plan of organizing groups of pupils to visit people of experience and knowledge in the neighbourhood to get first-hand information from them is the best. This has been very successful in many schools in the United Kingdom, and might be used widely in most countries; because adults ought to be called upon to help senior pupils to collect information, and to help them to make first-hand acquaintance with modern developments in all walks of life: in garages, shops, banks, farms and fisheries. The knowledge of the experts also is badly needed by young people so that they may learn about and preserve traditional customs and ways of working. Usually adults are very ready to provide help. The scheme has to be discussed fully in the classroom first, and various ways of securing accurate information is considered, and then precise arrangements are made by teacher and class together, or by a committee chosen by the class. As far as possible nothing should be left to chance, but all planned carefully; though there will be untoward incidents and unexpected developments and interesting results nevertheless.

When all the information possible has been gathered, it is written down by each group, then discussed and revised in class, and finally presented by the group as a report—a most valuable training for these senior pupils. But before the final revision of the reports, it is best to have at least one period in which the groups present a very informal account of their visits and enquiries, their difficulties and receptions. The children always enjoy this first meeting together, even if they have not been very successful, and it always has a great effect on the class, inspiring further plans and projects. If a project of this kind is planned round some of the careers open to the pupils, it will have a usefulness far beyond that of developing a sound mastery of a language: the subjects could be, for example, Life in a Hospital; The Duties of a Policeman; Work at a Civic Centre; The Post Office and How it is Organized; The Public Works Department.

Chapter 18

THE BEGINNINGS OF WRITTEN COMPOSITION

ALL classes should begin by writing compositions that keep very close to the content of lessons in their Readers. After a few weeks of this work an average class might pass on to writing about the subject-matter in the Reader but should include facts and ideas not in the Readers, such ideas as pupils can contribute from their everyday experience or reading or general knowledge. In the preparation for this, the class should be asked questions that are based on the text, but that seek for information not in the Reader: Stage Three Questions. These are asked in order to make the pupils think further about all that is mentioned in the text and what is related to it. They use the subject that has already been studied as a spring-board for diving into wider aspects of the subject. The class will already have some ideas about the subject, and will know many of the words that they will need. But the next step is a difficult one, for it is the expression of facts and ideas that hitherto has not been attempted, yet pupils who have been given good oral preparation should produce good work.

Much depends on the teacher's skill in questioning. At first, if good work is to follow without too many mistakes, the questions must keep to information about the subject that the class is likely to know. But if no one can explain some process or fact that occurs in their reading, for instance, how a gun works and how it fires (which most girls do not know), the teacher should pass on to other better understood points, for it will deflect the interest and aim of the lesson

if much new knowledge is to be imparted. Then in preparing to write about complicated processes, such as the
working of a steam-engine, each question should ask for one
point, and not for a series of actions or movements, as that
would be too much for many classes. For instance, the
questions should not ask how a steam-engine works; but
" If I put more coal on the fire under the engine, what
happens to the water in the boiler ? " To be pinned down
to a single detail like this ensures clear thinking; otherwise
boys who are not familiar with steam-engines, as many are
not, will have very confused or wrong ideas of how they
work. Nor should a question be vague, for instance, " What
happens ? " Instead, one simple question can lead on to
another until the whole process is clearly understood; for
instance, " What happens to the water when the fire is lit ? "
—" It gets hotter." " Right, and then what happens when
it boils ? "—" It bubbles and steam comes." " Right, and
what happens to the steam ? " In this way, by bringing in
precise details in the questions, a teacher can help his pupils
to give accurate and precise answers in correct English, and
in the correct order. And by splitting up a topic and asking
detailed questions one after the other, he helps his pupils to
note exactly what happens, and so to think clearly and
concretely.

This Stage Three Questioning should be thorough and
lively. It can be carried out at the end of a reading lesson
if there is time, or at the beginning of the composition period
after the reading has been done. It can call for longer and
longer answers as the class progresses, and so lead on to
Oral or Written Composition. In contrast to Stage Two
Questions, which are *intensive*, Stage Three Questions are
extensive. Stage Two keep closely to the content of the
passage read, and bring out the details of things mentioned

F

in the text. But Stage Three rove widely and freely over the whole field covered by the passage or chapter that has been read, and then even beyond that, touching on and throwing light over everything or anything related to the subject. This extensive questioning forces pupils to see where ideas and facts that they have come across are related to affairs of daily life and to outside school concerns of all sorts. They learn to make use of ideas that they have picked up, read about or have been taught. It is important for their educational progress that they do learn to range widely over a great variety of fact and experience.

In the writing about all that they have discussed and read, they are learning how to explain, to describe, to weigh up facts and evidence, opinion and fact. Their writing of compositions then teaches them *to handle ideas*. It teaches them how to express them and how to present them in an orderly and effective way. It should teach them to sort out the muddle and disorder of their thoughts and put these down on paper so that they are easy to understand, and so that they lead the reader on in an unbroken and logical line of thought. If it can do this, or some of it, it will also be teaching them to think, that is to say, to think clearly, to think logically and to think deeply. As they learn to handle ideas and to express them, their mastery of English also improves, and, what is more, becomes useful to them, helping them to reason, to judge, to enquire and to make logical deductions and to come to sound conclusions. If the children could have this kind of training in their mother tongue *as well*, their command and expression of ideas, and their ability to use their minds competently would have even greater stimulus. It is not the intelligence of our pupils that is not good enough, it is the training that is at fault.

Chapter 19

COMPOSITION: THE CHOICE OF SUBJECT

THE choice of a subject for either oral or written composition in a foreign tongue needs to be given especially careful thought. The reasons for this are that pupils should not have to face difficulties of subject matter as well as difficulties of language; and that the aim of this work in a foreign language is not to develop thought in unfamiliar subjects or copious ideas in a familiar one. A further reason is that composition in a new language is not intended to increase skill in setting out ideas in an effective order, or in building up a close series of arguments or in composing a reasoned treatment of some subject. Its purpose is to give practice in the expression of ideas and facts that the pupils have gathered for themselves. Composition in a new language, therefore, is *language practice*.

This practice is not merely to improve the use of new words and structures, though that is one of its purposes, it is to increase skill in handling the language; mainly the language that has already been acquired. This skill will be skill in using it clearly, in handling it correctly, and in making use of it with precision and effectiveness. Thus our pupils will learn how to use the language more effectively in description, that is, more accurately and vividly; more effectively in explanation, that is, more concretely and exactly; and more effectively in other uses of language, for instance, in communication, in entertainment, in persuasiveness, in reasoning.

First, then, we need subjects that will help pupils to learn to handle the language with ease and confidence. As we are not requiring them to display fresh ideas, or to write something that is particularly interesting, we can set them subjects that arise from their everyday lives. The purpose of this plan is that they will be so familiar with a set subject that there will not be the slightest difficulty, even for weak pupils, to produce ideas: they will all " have something to say." The virtue of this is that the pupils will not have to search for ideas at the same time as they are giving attention to correctness of language, good construction of sentences and other problems of expression. The ideas for them to express should be so readily flowing in their minds, and ready to be communicated, that they can give their full attention to the way that these ideas can be expressed.

We have always to remember that, in setting composition, we wish to give the children easy practice in good English. We are not trying to catch them out and to trap them into making mistakes (in order to find out that they do not know the grammar well enough), and we are not trying to see if they can use complex constructions correctly. We are trying to give them as much practice as possible in correct usages so that these may be firmly rooted in their linguistic habits. For the secret of really good language teaching is to arrange for endless practice in the correct forms and structures; and not to let pupils go blundering along trying to express what they do not really know—in a medium they have not really mastered ! Therefore we must avoid giving them subjects that invite mistakes; for instance, complicated problems such as the work of the Legislative Assembly, or vague theories such as What Steam has brought to Mankind, or unfamiliar knowledge and half-understood fact, such as The Provision and Purification of Water in Africa and India, A Sugar Refinery, or " Time."

The subjects for composition, therefore, except for reproduction and narrative, should at first be about the children's everyday lives, and only about events, happenings and incidents that the children know well. There is another reason for this: if they have clear and exact ideas, they will have less difficulty in finding the right words and the correct forms to express those ideas, than they would have had if their ideas had been vague or imperfectly grasped. Furthermore, as the children are more interested in what is actually going on around them than in general or ' book ' subjects, their ideas flow more freely, and with less confusion.

The need to choose subjects within the children's first-hand experience is particularly important for general progress in mastering a new language; for research on pupils' written compositions has discovered that the number of mistakes made by pupils varies according to the kind of subject they write about. It was found that the number of errors in pupils' compositions was much greater when they were writing on subjects about which they knew very little. But when they wrote about things they knew because they had seen them, such as " The Dress of your Chief " or because they had done them, such as " How do you clean your house ? ", the average number of mistakes in the compositions was very much less. Further research established the fact that when the children wrote about their everyday lives, they made far fewer mistakes—grammar, spelling, vocabulary—than when they wrote on subjects that they had been studying in school, that had been learnt from their Readers, or from their teacher's notes and explanations. For instance, it was found that when pupils of about thirteen and fourteen wrote on the subject of ' Hygiene,' after they had had instruction on it and had read a chapter about it, the percentage of correct sentences in the work of the whole form was only 20; but when the same pupils wrote about their daily duties at home, the percentage of correct sentences ranged from 38 to 43. And the compositions written from the pupils' own experience were more interesting and more exact, with better continuity and less confusion of thought. Further counting of thousands of mistakes provided convincing evidence that the language was always better and more correct when writers knew a good deal about the subject of their compositions.

Still further study of the problem brought to light the fact that the proportion of incorrect sentences went up when pupils attempted general subjects, such as ' Beasts of Burden,' or ' Travel,' or ' The Sea.' This kind of subject, which was so popular in England in the first quarter of the twentieth century, encourages children to make vague statements and unsound deductions, such as " The chief beast of burden is the horse "—most of them perhaps never having seen a horse, or only such knobbly, skin-clothed skeletons that could hardly be recognised as horses. Sometimes, too, many of the writers would often bring in statements that were not true, in order to fill out the composition.

Subjects of a general nature do not usually stimulate exact thinking, because pupils have not as a rule the groundwork of fact and knowledge that is the necessary material to think with. In this matter we do not always realize that to form deductions, to draw conclusions, to follow up relationships with other things, processes and events, we need facts and knowledge about the world we know best. But general subjects can suggest to most pupils only vague and general ideas; for very few pupils realize that a general subject can be, and usually should be, dealt with by concentrating on particulars. In order to learn how to treat a general subject by dealing concretely with a small part of it, most pupils would need many examples and careful training.

The best subjects, then, are those that are particular, limited, concrete and realistic. Therefore, instead of setting a subject like " Village Life," which appears to be satisfactory as it is concrete and realistic, the title should be " Life in My Village." Instead of " Travel in My Country," the subject should be " A Lorry (or Train) Journey from My Town to the Capital "—often the more particular and limited it is the better. So instead of " Your Town," which for most pupils is no more limited than " Town Life," the subject could be " What I see in the Main Street of My Town." Thus, at the beginning of composition work, and for all weak pupils throughout, the title should nearly always contain some definite and limiting words, such as ' in the High Street ': that will help the pupils to concentrate on one important scene, and to describe that with plenty of detail. The title, then, should help the young writers to think of and imagine one thing at a time, and to write about that fully and vividly, thereby saving them from wandering on and just touching on a number of points. If a title helps them to attend to one thing, it will also promote relevance, continuity and concreteness: all of which are difficult to produce in pupils' compositions, just as it is to achieve in one's own. We ought to remember here the advice that a wise teacher once wrote: " Choose titles which give not a wide but a small target."[1]

There are other subjects that research has shown to be unsatisfactory. For instance, the subject " Pets," and similar topics, are quite unsuitable for pupils in countries where the keeping of pets is almost unknown. For a similar reason subjects like " Hobbies," " Stamp-Collecting," and

---

[1] *Learning Our Language.* D. Benzies. (Longmans, Green.)

" Model-Making," though frequently set, are unsuitable for many countries; though such subjects might be satisfactory in secondary schools of the grammar school type.

It was discovered, too, that proverbs, such as " A stitch in time saves nine," or sayings like " Mind your own business " nearly always produced very poor work, full of vague statements and insincere moralizings, or else they trapped pupils into telling a story which seemed to illustrate the title, but which actually had nothing to do with it. Subjects that were dealt with in the pupils' Reader, such as " A Journey to the Moon," often produced only very poor reproductions of what was in the Reader. Subjects dealing with games, like " A Football Match," were nearly always done very badly. This subject is too complicated, for too many small actions happen in a very short time, and it is very difficult to make an account full enough. In fact, this subject is often too difficult for English pupils to do well in their mother tongue, although it appears to be a good one for them. It would be better to set " How I scored the Winning Goal "; but even that will produce journalese and clichés. Other unsuitable subjects were noted, such as " The Sun," " The Wild Animals in My Country " (very few pupils in some countries know enough about the animals to write about them).

The subjects that produced the best work were as follows:—" Firewood: Gathering, Carrying and Storing "; " What we use Pestle and Mortar for, and how we use them "; " Repairing Huts and Walls "; " Making a Fence "; " Games we play at home "; " What I do on Saturdays "; " What happens at the Well (or Water-Tap) "; " What we do when we go bathing "; " What a good lorry-driver does "; " How to make and look after a garden "; " I visit a Market "; " How to make pots (baskets, mats, nets . . .) ";

" How to make Soap "; " Catching a chicken and preparing it for the pot." These subjects, of course, reflect the daily lives of pupils in parts of West Africa, so they will not necessarily be suitable for other parts of Africa or other countries: the principle in choosing subjects is that these should always reflect the life of the children, except those for the top classes.

Chapter 20

CORRECTING COMPOSITIONS

THE correction of compositions can help a pupil to learn a new language, instead of merely showing him and his teacher what he does not know, or his own carelessness. But if the correcting is to be really helpful, learners must acquire the habit of noticing mistakes in their own writing and speaking. This habit can be acquired fairly early if the language learners are properly trained. They need to acquire, too, the habit of feeling responsible for corrections and for their own use of the language. Consequently if teachers will develop these habits in their pupils, they will be giving them valuable help towards final success.

The training that will help pupils to become aware of their mistakes and to feel responsible for them has to be gradual and continuous. It is quite easy to carry out, it saves a great deal of time, and it can help the pupils to write the foreign language with increasing correctness. For whenever pupils are being taught to find and correct their own mistakes, they are receiving an effective exercise in applying the grammar that they have learnt. And such a grammar exercise is focused on the forms and usages that they do not know well enough, and so additional grammar application exercises are often not needed. Correcting one's own mistakes is the best kind of grammar-application exercise that can be devised, because it forces the pupil to notice the correct forms, and it makes him feel responsible or the correcting. Even if many pupils do not acquire this habit completely, or sometimes do not alter mistakes correctly, the task of looking for them helps to draw attention to the spellings and forms and structures that they are learning. This practical plan has much to recommend it, yet it has been much neglected, or used only half-heartedly.

Not only must this training in looking for and correcting mistakes be gradually more strict, it must also be varied, and it should not make too many demands on the pupils at first. Unlike pronunciation, many mistakes may be missed and remain uncorrected by the pupils, and no harm is done. Pupils beginning this task cannot find all their mistakes; nevertheless, with persistence, improvement will come, even if slowly.

We have to realize that when the teacher marks all the mistakes in his pupils' compositions, the pupils are not being taught to notice incorrect forms, so they go on using them. And when a teacher writes in all of the corrections, the pupils are not receiving any practice in using the correct forms and expressions that they did not know, but the teacher is ! But what is worse, the effect of the teacher's work on the pupils is usually very small; indeed, on many of them there will be none. So the teacher has expended much effort and care, and time, too, with too little result. If the effect of his marking and entries in the books had been good, the effort would have been worth while; but the result on the pupils' learning very very rarely justifies the long time spent on the correcting, especially with large classes. And the more conscientious the teacher or the more insistent the Head to have every single mistake corrected, the greater the effort and the longer the time; but how far do the results justify this expenditure ?

Even if pupils have to copy out a fair version of their corrected work, the effect is still small, because most copying out is done mechanically, or almost mechanically, little note being taken of the correct forms that had not been known. Well-established mistakes can never be eradicated in that way. But obviously something must be done : pupils cannot go on making mistakes without being corrected. Some teachers insist on the pupils' writing in the corrections. That is a good method; but if the teacher has found all the mistakes and suggests all the corrections, then there is no urgency for the pupils to learn the correct forms and grammar, so they may never learn them. But there *should* be an urgency—if the pupil is to learn the language.

There is another good reason why pupils should be made to find their own mistakes and correct them: research has revealed that very many grammatical and spelling mistakes in children's writing are the result, not of lack of knowledge, but of *carelessness*. This was an astonishing discovery; but it can easily be tested by asking any class to supply the correct forms for mistakes that have been made in the last piece of composition: it surprises most teachers to find how many can be produced by the pupils who have made the mistakes.

Special measures will be needed to ensure that the pupils are forming habits of responsibility for their work, and of feeling some pride in turning out careful work. It need not be assumed that this plan will mean more work for the teacher; on the contrary, soon after the training has commenced, the teacher will find that he has less correcting to do, and that his marking of written work takes less time. The better he trains his pupils, the less work he will have to do in the marking, so there is a gain here for the teacher, as well as for the pupil; and there is also more likelihood of the teacher being fresh and energetic for the harder but more important work of intensive oral questioning.

What is the effect on a pupil's learning of his writing in the corrections ? By having to write in the correct version, the pupil is left with the correct usage in mind; whereas if the teacher corrects a mistake, the pupil who has used the incorrect form, may still have that in mind, for the correct form has not necessarily replaced the incorrect one. The correction was made on paper, and may have made no impression at all on the incorrect usage that is still fixed in the pupil's mind. It is the pupil's mental habit that needs correcting, not the writing on the paper !

Also, in learning languages, it is not enough to know the grammar: the pupil has to be able to *use* it, to apply it, to make his thought keep to the correct forms: it is not a question of words and inflections, etc., it is a question of mental habits, of the pupil's mental habits using the correct forms and structures: that's where we so often go wrong. It is not enough to know, for the learner's intellectual knowledge does not automatically determine his physical and natural use of the language. It is not enough, for instance, for him to know that in English a Plural Noun must be followed by the Plural form of the Verb when he uses the Present Tense. What is necessary is that his speech habits after saying " Boys . . ." must automatically be forming the sounds " have . . ." or " are . . ." Because it is the pattern of *sound* " Boys have . . ." or " Boys are . . ." and of muscular movements of his speech organs that have to be fixed habits. The pattern of meanings which he thinks and of sounds that he makes has to be an automatic linguistic reaction. Similarly, the pattern " Each of the boys " must be automatically followed by " has " and not by " have." So it is the mental habit that needs to be corrected—and the correct forms usually have to be ' drilled in ' if mistakes have been made. But when a teacher has found " Boys has . . ." or " Each of the boys have . . ." and has corrected it, and the pupil has done nothing, the error must surely persist as a linguistic pattern in his speech habits, even if he might have known intellectually what the mistake was. It is only the pupil's mental and physical repetitions that will eradicate the error from his linguistic habits if it is firmly rooted there.

Now it takes time to train young pupils to find and correct their mistakes; but most children can learn to do this accurately enough to justify the method. It has been tried out in several schools in the Gold Coast in very different areas, as well as in the United Kingdom, and it has been found that it helps pupils to write more correctly, and that they find interest in doing corrections in that way.

In carrying out the training a teacher should include some or all of the following, or his own variations of them:—

(a) All pupils read through their own written work before handing it in, and correct any mistakes they can find. At first they will not find many, but with a little urging, and the teacher's going round and pointing to lines where he can see one, more will always be found. The habit of revising written work like this is a useful one to inculcate, though it may irk the careless pupil. When it has become a habit, it is far less trouble. It is one that many of us have to acquire.

(b) In the lower classes the correct answers to exercises may often be written on the board, and then the children can correct the sentences themselves. This is good for their learning, because then they should make no mistakes in their corrections, nor should they miss any. Those that happen to be missed or that are altered incorrectly must be written in correctly by the pupils; if the teacher does it, the usefulness of writing the answers on the board is lost. It is usually better to write up the answers than to dictate them, because young children are usually not capable of listening attentively to small details for more than a few minutes, and often they do not hear the correct version, and so mistakes occur. Answers should be dictated perhaps only to senior pupils, or when time is short.

(c) Whenever pupils are writing, a teacher can walk round, looking through the work they have done, and putting a small cross at the end of those lines which contain a mistake. The children then have to find a mistake on that line and correct it, so the simple task is easy for them. When the teacher comes round again, he puts a tick through the cross if the mistake has been altered correctly; if not he leaves the cross. This takes very little time, because he does not spend long at each desk; if he is quick, he can get an exercise almost completely corrected. With large classes or senior pupils who write more, he might get at least half an exercise corrected.

(d) The well-known plan of putting signs in the column opposite mistakes in compositions is perhaps more suited to secondary grammar school work and for longer compositions of the senior class. In this, instead of a cross, the different kinds of mistake are indicated by different signs, for instance, S—spelling; P—punctuation; T—wrong Tense; W—word wrongly used; N—mistake of Number. The teacher using this marking scheme has to go round the class in order to see if mistakes have been corrected, or has to look through the books later. If some mistakes are missed, it does not always matter, because we cannot expect perfection at this stage in such work. But if the signs help to increase the pupils' care and attention, the pupils are benefiting from the scheme.

(*e*) When written work has to be handed in, the teacher can say: " Read through your work and count up your mistakes. Put the number you have found at the bottom of the page. Then correct them." He might give the class three minutes for this, going round as many as he can, pointing at lines where mistakes have been missed. The books are then collected, and when he corrects them he puts the number of mistakes he finds at the bottom of the page. This is continued for two weeks or more, the pupils trying to score the same number as the teacher.

(*f*) The procedure just described may then be varied, though only small variations will be necessary to keep interest in this new game of hunt the error. The first variation might spring a surprise on the class by the teacher saying, when they have corrected all the mistakes they have found, " Now read through your work again, and see if you can find some more mistakes. Put the new number at the bottom of the page." They usually find several more mistakes without the teacher's help. Then he can suggest that they try to reduce their scores and to find them all on the first reading through. Later, he can say: " Change books with your neighbour. Mark his mistakes, putting the number of them at the bottom as usual." When they have finished: " Hand books back and correct the mistakes that have been marked. See if you can find some that your neighbour has missed." Thus he varies the procedure, keeping the class guessing about what he will want them to do; and so he stimulates his pupils to keep a sharp eye for mistakes and keen to keep the number they score as low as possible. Other variations may suggest themselves as the work goes on.

(*g*) For the sake of completeness it might be mentioned that the method of correcting exercises by using the Reader, each pupil checking his own exercise and looking up Tenses, spelling, etc., and correcting a whole exercise, should be used as often as possible.

In all of this work, if a teacher goes round, helping his pupils by asking them questions to get them to remember correct grammar, if he interests them in the problem of correcting compositions and explains to them why it will help their learning of the language, if he practises them in finding correct spellings from their Readers and dictionaries, if he gets them to keep progress charts or graphs of the numbers of their mistakes, or carries out other little devices and schemes like that, the training in polishing up compositions will be more successful. If much of this is done, a fair copy will often not be needed. And in going round a class the teacher will soon be able to see which are the commonest mistakes, and will then make up exercises to combat the chief weaknesses. The underlying principle is that the responsibility for correctness should be the pupil's, as far as possible—not solely the teacher's.

Chapter 21

HOW CAN PUPILS' COMPOSITIONS
BE IMPROVED ?

AFTER his pupils have been writing continuous compositions for a year or more, a teacher should be asking himself: " How can I raise the general standard of my pupils' compositions ? " He will not find the answer easily; and the problem of raising ' poor ' compositions to the level of ' average ' is just as difficult as raising the ' average ' ones to the ' good ' grade. The problem is complicated because there are at least four main aspects to deal with: ideas, and their arrangement, the language, and its correctness. But the real difficulty is that a teacher will often not know what kind of help will enable his pupils to write better. For instance, will they be helped by instruction, by criticism, by praise, by examples of good writing, or by better preparation ? Of course, some of these ways might help one pupil, and others might help other pupils. How is a teacher to find out how to bring about improvement ? The difficulty is to discover a way that is simple, easy to understand and effective.

The way to set about discovering what to do is, however, comparatively simple, though to succeed in this needs patience and true interest in the problem, as well as careful thought. The way to success in this task is through literary diagnosis: the teacher has to find out first what weaknesses can be detected in his pupils' compositions. He must diagnose before he can apply remedies. He has to study the written work and to examine it critically so as to find out where and in what respect improvement is needed. This is not such a difficult task as it may seem; though to give a number of compositions a careful scrutiny does need perseverance. The teacher may very soon see where weakness lies and this diagnosis may be confirmed in the next few compositions. One way to find weakness is to question each composition as one reads: " Are there too few ideas here, or is the expression too vague and inexact ? "—" Are the ideas too general and sweeping, and not detailed enough ? "—" Are related ideas linked by connecting words ? "—" Does the thought jump from fact to fact without any understandable connections or logical sequence ? "—" Are the ideas good, but jumbled in the wrong order ? " With questions like these in mind as one reads, it is often easy to perceive where pupils need help.

There are six aspects of children's written work that often need special attention. These are: grammatical correctness, the content and ideas in the writing, the relevance of ideas to subject, the continuity of language and of thought, the orderly arrangement of ideas, and the expression of these ideas and how far such expression is effective in carrying out the writer's intention. The suggestions that follow are not necessarily better than other ways of dealing with weakness in written work; if they fail, other ways must be tried.

(i) **Grammatical Correctness.** The results of research on the problem of grammatical mistakes in written work might be useful as a rough guide for teachers. It is evident that if the average number of grammatical mistakes in written work is high, then there is special weakness in *applying* the grammar learned. Therefore some figures were worked out by counting the grammar mistakes in hundreds of compositions written by pupils who had been writing English for three, four or five years. It was estimated that if most of the pupils in a class had an average of two or more grammatical mistakes per line in their free written English, then a term's course of supplementary grammar exercises should be given, in addition to the regular oral and written grammar work. These exercises should be all written, and should require the *use* of the grammar in sentences and short paragraphs. But if most of the pupils had an average of one mistake per line, or one in every two lines, then these additional grammar exercises should be given two days a week, instead of every day. If, however, there was an average of only one mistake in every three lines in a pupil's writing, then there was no special weakness in grammar in the written work.

To effect lasting improvement in this category of weakness, pupils have to be trained to feel responsible for their work, and for finding most of their mistakes: no other remedy is so effective. In addition, it is best to find out which are the most prevalent mistakes of each class, and to concentrate the grammar exercises on those, rather than to bring in all sorts of grammar practice. In order to discover the most frequent mistakes the counting method should be used, because it is the comparative frequency in each category that has to be estimated. It is a good plan, and often more effective than anything else in producing improvement, to allow pupils to do the counting and to keep the records, and to let a senior pupil, or the most troublesome boy, log the totals each week. This engages interest and produces more careful writing. But extra instruction that merely explains grammatical rules and usages is unlikely to have sufficient effect on prevalent mistakes to be worth while.

(ii) **Good and Plentiful Ideas.** If half the pupils in a class produce only very short compositions, or if longer compositions contain many dull statements and only general references to definite things, it may be that the preparation for writing is too short, too general or too remote from the children's lives. To improve the preparation is easy: questions should be more detailed, their number increased, and the teacher's suggestions should be reduced in number, for they have not been helping the pupils very much. The fault may be in the choice of subject, so a more suitable and interesting selection might help.

The lack of stimulating questions is often the cause of feeble written work. Perhaps it is not realized that questions may be searching, and should drive the pupils to remember all they have known about a subject, not merely what they have heard recently or read in school; and they should help the pupils to imagine the events or things they are to write about vividly and in exact detail. Improvement will nearly always follow when a teacher makes the minds of his pupils actively interested in real life; but if he relies on himself to produce the ideas and information for the compositions, no good progress in writing is usually possible.

Children's minds can be made alert and interested in various ways, sometimes by trying one way and sometimes another—variety is a good spice in intellectual as well as in physical nourishment. The children's minds can be stimulated by various means: (a) by questioning that is energetic and focused on well-known details; (b) by reading aloud to the class from interesting books; (c) by encouraging a class to collect information in various ways; (d) by promoting good story-telling; (e) by lively acting, play-making, or by puppet-plays; (f) by the pupils reading more; (g) by having 'General Knowledge' periods once a week, and perhaps a competitive period for forms in pairs during the last hour on Friday afternoon; (h) by having occasional talks on subjects of topical interest, perhaps given by a teacher to several forms at once.

Thus in many ways a wide variety of subject can be enquired into, investigated and discussed by a class; and some subjects can be properly 'worked up' ready for written work, and the children incited to find out things for themselves, especially to look up subjects and facts in books. Much can be done incidentally in conversations with pupils outside the classroom, and what a teacher does incidentally often has more effect on a pupil than all that he has told him in class. If a teacher can fire his pupils to show initiative in the search for knowledge, without too much reliance on him, so that the pupils become curious to understand many things, he will be doing far more for them than could normally be done in ordinary school work.

(iii) **Continuity of Language and Thought.**   When writing narrative, most pupils can soon improve their work by being trained to keep in mind the exact order of the actions in the story. Frequent emphasis on this during oral preparation for story-telling will help, and insistence on pupils examining their own writing to see what order they have given to the action will make them aware of the necessity for continuity. All that the young writers have to do is to imagine the actions as they would occur in real life, and make sure that no gap is left in the train of thought. Similarly in writing about how machines work and in explaining how to make things and how to do different kinds of work, such as washing clothes, building a house, clearing the ground for yam or corn growing, pupils can soon see where there is a gap in what is being done, and this will usually indicate a lack of continuity, and perhaps that some point has been left out.

Improvement in continuity can often be achieved by the pupils making plans for their writing, and by their examining the headings of the plan to see that they lead on in a connected sequence. They should be able to see when they have made too big a stride in thought or a sideways jump on to some unrelated topic.

Improvement can sometimes be obtained by asking questions in the oral preparation stage that keep very strictly to an obvious order of events, or steps in an explanation of some process, such as making charcoal or a dress. This close sequence can be indicated in the plan on the board, and this plan used as an example of continuity in a composition. The frequent question when plans are being compiled on the board should be " Can we make any improvements on the order of these notes and headings ? " A regular question of this kind is often much more effective in driving a point home than frequent general reminders or repeated instructions, which lose their power the more often they are heard. It is also a useful type of question because it helps to train the senior pupils to think of facts, information, etc., as material to be arranged and to be manipulated, and then brought into their compositions in an intelligent way, not just included as they are thought of or remembered.

(iv) **Clarity of Language.** Improvement in clarity of language is not easy to bring about; for it is useless to *tell* a class to write clearly, though some teachers have a habit of impressing on their classes that they must do such things. It is useless because those who do not write clearly do not usually know what clear writing is, or what they should do to write like that. It is often easy for us to recognize clear writing, but not easy to explain what clear writing is. Some other method must be found to replace the lazy and ineffective method of talking to a class about clear writing.

The three following ways of helping pupils to write clearly have been found effective. The class can be shown on the board examples of short explanations, and pupils called on to find where ideas are muddled or too vague, and then asked for alterations, and finally the class can be asked to choose the clearest of these. The class can be practised in finding unclear expression in their own writings, and in making suggestions for improvements. The teacher can question the class more precisely than usual whenever they are to write on complicated or confusing subjects, such as " What happens when gears are changed in driving a lorry ? " This questioning in the preparation stage can often help pupils to think clearly by making them attend to exact details one at a time. Then their writing may improve. There is no point in telling pupils to bring in details; the questions must ensure that they do so.

(v) **Relevance to Subject.** Research into pre-secondary school composition writing revealed that irrelevance was a common weakness. It was found that many pupils wrote quite good English, but spoilt their work by dragging in facts and ideas that had nothing to do with the subject they were writing about; sometimes even pious warnings were included. A study of large numbers of compositions showed that, even when pupils made a good plan of the points to be included in their compositions, they often failed to follow this plan, and so it had very little effect on the compositions. It did not keep out irrelevances, because the pupils apparently took very little notice of it. It appeared that pupils often included sentences in their compositions that were completely irrelevant in order to make up the number of lines they were expected to produce, or to fill up the page. The remedy for this weakness is simple: pupils must keep to the plans they make. And if they have to underline all the irrelevant sentences in their own compositions before handing them in, this curious habit might be eradicated.

The examination of these compositions also proved that when children wrote about what they knew well, and what they did and saw in their daily lives, there was very much less irrelevance: thus a better choice of subject might also help to cure irrelevant writing.

Chapter 22

THE FOREIGN LANGUAGE IN THE LAST YEARS OF SCHOOL

PUPILS at the top of the school are looking forward very often to a new life and other interests: consequently school events and ambitions that have loomed so large hitherto now fade into the background, and no longer tempt these pupils to put their whole heart into the work and their play, or into other school activities. Those few that have some small responsibilities and school duties still have something to occupy their minds and attention; but most of the others in the top classes will often find little to interest them in their last school year. Furthermore, these pupils are rapidly growing to maturity, and many of them will feel that school no longer has much to offer them. They do not find in their textbooks new ideas and new knowledge shedding light on hitherto partially understood subjects, for these textbooks usually have little to interest or to help these pupils. Even if there are special textbooks for them, these often offer too little as far as these pupils' real personal needs are concerned. And what is more regrettable, sometimes a top class has to work again through the book used during the previous year, so that there is nothing at all fresh, nothing for them to get their sharpening intellectual teeth into, nothing to lure them on to attack new problems or to master new knowledge. This is a deplorable state of affairs. Too little thought has been given to this problem; it is a serious one, for it affects very many good pupils; it needs imaginative planning to handle this difficulty with courage and understanding.

This is not the place to suggest drastic remedies; but the teachers of English can always do something to help, even in the most difficult circumstances. These pupils need, for instance, a specially devised and ambitiously planned programme for their language work. They should have had, of course, the promise of some special work held out to them when they were approaching the end of the previous year; and they should have been warned that the plan would require hard work on their part, but that it would do something to prepare them for the future. Now what could be devised ?

The plan could include a study (mainly reading and discussion) of topics in everyday life that a young man or young woman should know something about; for example, the Red Cross and its work, the Social Services, government —policies, administration, organization, and especially local government, the running of the postal services, public libraries, public utility services, civic responsibilities, the duties of the Public Works Department, etc. There is plenty for them to study. These subjects could be studied for themselves in English lessons, and the ordinary school English lesson abandoned, except when there was a need for further instruction and for practice on special points—a need that often arises. Formal instruction in English could take a back place; but the pupils' command of the language would improve because the new interests would foster the use of more purposive language than might be possible in formal work, and the pupils' minds might well be more alive and quicker to learn. Thus the practice in language that the pupils would now get would be more definite and more exact than it could have been if the ordinary school work had been continued.

It would be part of this new plan of course to promote wider and more intelligent reading. A special lesson might profitably be used to explain the new reading programme, and the new tasks that each pupil or group would be required to undertake. New and more exacting projects than hitherto would be outlined, discussed and carefully planned by the class, with the various responsibilities apportioned. Pupils could be made responsible for reading selected books, for reporting on them and describing their contents and value. This part of the project could be done orally or in writing, and, if worth while, summaries of the most useful information in them could be written and then discussed. Each reader or group could be given the responsibility for recommending the books they were given to read, or of reporting on them adversely. When others of the class had read some of those that had been recommended, the discussion might be more fruitful and keener than usual, and such critical questions as the following might be fired at the reader responsible: " Why was this book thought to be good enough for us all to read ? "—" Why were not these points put forward by the reader of that book ? Were they missed or only thought to be of little importance ? "

Similar projects could be carried out on magazines, newspapers, official pamphlets and school textbooks. Discussion on all this reading material could be sharpened by keen questioning on details in the books: this would force readers to read with attention to exact detail. Each reporting session would best be carried out on formal lines, with pupil chairman to control the questioning. The written reports could provide some of the most useful written work that the class would do. In this kind of programme it would be the teacher's aim to stimulate the work, to present tasks that were useful, and to exact high standards in the reading, the discussions and in the reporting. His general aim might be to make the pupils not only work, but work hard and willingly, and to give them responsibility for the work of the whole class.

The independent reading of these pupils should also be extended and encouraged: books that might satisfy their interests and needs for entertainment as well as for information should be recommended and, if possible, sampled. Books that might help them in various ways after they have left school should be made known to them, and be read by some of them, in whole or in part. These pupils should at least know what kinds of book are available, and what books might be especially useful to them in their future work. They should dip into a number of subjects that are closely related to occupations that may be open to them after leaving school; such as building, economics, surveying, engineering, agriculture, mining, and trades like printing, dyeing, papermaking, etc.

In addition to this somewhat utility reading, other books, less technical, should be dipped into or read all through by all or some of the class. In this plan, the less usual subjects should be looked into, read up carefully and discussed in class. Subjects like astronomy and perhaps astrology, zoology and biology, pottery and glass-work, physics and chemistry, medicine and surgery, and many of the applied arts and sciences, could be introduced to a class by individuals or groups reading simple introductions to the subject. The best classes would enjoy some simple philosophy. If a teacher knew little or less about some subject, that would not matter in the least; in fact, it might be an advantage, for then he could join in the discovery of knowledge. He might tell the class what it is that interests him in a subject, and some of the pupils, previously unwilling to work hard, might delve into a subject solely for the purpose of passing over some information to the teacher: a proposal that would attract a certain kind of pupil, and then perhaps win his co-operation. In this case, the teacher could turn the tables by questioning pupils like this in order to force them to get up their information more fully and precisely: if this were done with a sincere desire to help them to learn more about some subject, it would be most stimulating to a top class of maturing boys.

If some simple projects and schemes like these were run on formal lines, and a class persuaded to produce a formal report on its findings, it might put some very hard work into the reading, compiling of notes and writing. The reports could be compiled under such titles as " Careers offering opportunities for young men (or young women) "; " Careers requiring special qualifications "; " Occupations with seasonal vacancies," and so on. If these reports were well done, some good writing practice would have been achieved and some really useful information collected and presented in a readable form. It should normally be the aim of the teacher to lead the work towards some kind of writing, as that consolidates thought, and gives opportunities for improving the pupils' handling of the language. To pin down the pupils to the recording of facts and the simple expression of information would be an admirable opportunity for teaching them the difference between clear, exact writing, and vague generalizations and abstractions.

In such ways as these, some very valuable work could be achieved. If the teacher exacts a really high standard, and manages to coax the writers to read their own writing critically and to try to improve it, some quite good writing might be achieved. If pupils could see when their writing was good, and why it was good, it would teach them a lesson in achievement, in perseverance and hard work, that would be of permanent value to them throughout their lives.

Chapter 23

PROBLEMS IN TEACHING LITERATURE

1. **The Use of Simplified Versions.** A clear distinction must be made between the version that *simplifies* the text of a book of literary standing and the version that *shortens* it only. The version that simplifies a text changes the more difficult (and often the more expressive) words and phrases for simpler (and therefore often feebler) words and expressions. The version that only shortens cuts out all that might be spared without reducing the value of the book *as literature* (or without reducing the value very much); so words, phrases, sentences and even paragraphs sometimes are left out if they can easily be spared, but difficult words and phrases are not changed. This distinction is most important; because it indicates a difference in the purpose and value of the two versions: the simplified version is excellent material for language learning, but not as literature; the shortened version is excellent material for language work and as literature.

The simplified series of classical novels and other well-known books have the virtues usually of a good story. The interest of a good story makes them good material for language learning, for new words and expressions are encountered, and can often be understood solely from the context, and the reader's mind becomes more and more accustomed to the syntax and structural patterns of the new language. But these simplified versions cannot have the special virtues of good literature—those virtues that are especially necessary for the finer education and full growth of intellect and emotion, and for the spiritual development of growing pupils who are passing through adolescence into a tender and vulnerable maturity.

In these simplified series the qualities of good literature have been so much watered down that they are less vivid, less interesting, less penetrating, and also less precise and true. The reason for all this is that simplified language has not the expressiveness, and the vitality or power of moving us, of stimulating the imagination, and of so holding our attention that we must participate in the adventures of the hero or heroine. And, therefore, however good these books are for language practice and reading, they can never give us just that particular value that good literature can.

But these simplified series are very useful for teaching reading. They can usually be read easily enough for pupils to enjoy reading them, and so they provide good material for developing the reading skills. And pupils that read enough of them, perhaps more than five a year, will usually acquire good reading habits, and possibly a love of reading— an end much to be desired and sought. In addition, the more these pupils are caught by the interest and perhaps the excitement of the story, the more firmly will the meanings of the words, as well as their correct usages, be impressed on their minds. They will also come across many new ideas, which they will assimilate; and so their general education will gain from their reading. It is essential for pupils to be encouraged, and even pressed to read these books, and to go on reading them after they have left school. If they continue to read, even only a few books every year, all the ground that has been gained and all the progress in language learning that they had achieved, will not be lost or the output of effort wasted. It has not been widely enough or strongly enough impressed on all language learners that

G

regular and constant reading of easy narrative will not only maintain the command of language that has been achieved, but can increase it.

The Use of Shortened Versions of Prose Literature. The reading of shortened versions of good prose literature will provide the language practice and training in the reading skills that we have referred to in the previous section; but in addition these versions can make a special contribution to pupils' education. They can make this contribution, however, only if the pupils read them with attention and imagination.

The value of good literature in the education of children is often referred to, but it is perhaps too often taken on trust. It might be useful, therefore, if we could perceive more clearly why good literature is included in educational programmes and considered to be important for school children. It may help us also to understand why " to be able to read good literature " is usually given as one of the chief reasons for teaching and learning foreign languages.

It will not be possible to deal here with all the reasons why literature is valuable in educating children, even if they were all known, because aesthetic values are too complex and obscure to be considered briefly. To assess the values of literature in the forming of ideals, standards of conduct and social attitudes would need reference to philosophy and psychology, and would require almost another book, as well as greater experience and competence in that field of learning. Nevertheless we can examine some of the less obscure points, for instance: literature is valuable for its language, for the ideas expressed and for the knowledge and insight that it can give.

Literature is valuable for its language. The learner of the language, in reading literature, is profiting from the clearest, most significant and the most appropriate use of words possible. The result of this reading experience is that he becomes more certainly aware of their fullest and richest meanings. He thus may learn to use these words himself more effectively, and also more appropriately in different contexts: he sees that this context demands this word, but not that; and this word is more suitable or more forcible in this context, but not in that.

At an earlier stage in learning a language, the value of the language of good literature to the learner is that it produces more distinct and more vivid descriptions, narrative, dialogue, consequently the meanings of the words become more distinctly and surely impressed on the mind, and there is more complete understanding. If pupils persist, reading often and with some enjoyment or even with avidity, improvement in understanding will certainly increase, and after a time should favourably affect their own use of language in speaking and writing.

The reason for this increase and deepening of understanding is that attention is held by interest in all that is happening, by a feeling of concern in the fate and actions of the characters, and by the excitement of the dangers and difficulties of these characters. The result is that the whole force of the mind and its now more active imagination are focused on meanings, on what the words are expressing; for the reader wants to know what happens next, and he has nothing else to tell him, except the words. He must inevitably understand more completely, and often even more forcibly. His emotion, his excitement and his curiosity drive him to seize every meaning and suggestion that the words can give him.

This imagined reality of character, action and dialogue is not achieved usually by ordinary narrative or by novels that are not considered to be ' good literature.' This is because the language is not expressive enough to affect us as good literature does. For when we read good literature we feel that the characters are of some importance to us, we enter into their lives, understanding their motives, desires and fears, and we feel as if we were personally concerned in their fate. All this is brought about by the writer's skill in language. It is the language that makes us imagine vividly and feel deeply, indeed, it compels us to do so, if we keep our minds focused on all that the words suggest to us. In return, this imagining and deep feeling about the characters keep our minds fully awake and ready to receive all that there is in the words.

The Value of Literature for its Ideas. Taking ourselves as simple examples, most of us have no doubt gathered a great deal of information about eighteenth and early nineteenth century life in England from the novels of Jane Austen, about Victorian England from Trollope, about country life and radical politics from George Eliot—and such ideas, for instance, as the customs, beliefs, habits, social attitudes and thought in those times, and especially ways of life. So our pupils in reading books that " hold, as 'twere, the mirror up to nature " will pick up a very great deal incidentally. Our pupils, for instance, when they read *Treasure Island* learn what is just and right when innkeepers are in difficulties, what is good discipline, the necessity for co-operation, even among buccaneers, and other ideas of social conduct. These ideas, of course, are not learnt consciously, nor need there be any questioning to see if pupils have assimilated them. They appeal to the imagination and are grasped intuitively, and so are assented to and accepted without question as being right and natural in the circumstances portrayed in the book—for this is ' truth ' and

' truth to nature,' which cannot be rejected by a sincere reader, however young, if the circumstances portrayed have been honestly imagined by the writer.

Such ideas and many others of all kinds are acquired by pupils during the reading of good literature: this is one reason why it is called ' good '—because it is rich in ideas that fertilize the thinking of many different kinds of men and women. These ideas contribute to the general stock of knowledge that every reader is accumulating when he is deeply absorbed in a well-told story. For good literature does not only give factual knowledge and objective information about characters and plot; it gives also deeper and more valuable ideas: ideas and thoughts and the moral teaching of society that concern the development of the pupils' characters, their outlook on life and their understanding of right conduct in human affairs.

The Value of Literature that gives insight into Human Nature. In reading novels we see how life is lived by different kinds of men and women, for we see it imaginatively as if enacted before us. We see how life must be faced by people in various situations and in very varied circumstances, often by people who meet with unexpected difficulties, who face disappointment, loss and danger. We learn how people stand up to and sometimes overcome the blows of bad fortune and the ugly spite of intrigue or underhand revenge; and we wonder how those who have won our admiration will face life when it threatens them so inescapably. With what courage, what loyalty and good humour do they sustain their hearts? How do they bear themselves ? And what happens to them: do they give in or give up, or do they go on unflinchingly until the end, an end which may be tragic ? Let us think of the characters that a boy will admire in the books he reads: Jim Hawkins in *Treasure Island*, Sidney

Carton in *A Tale of Two Cities*, Denys the Burgundian cross-bowman in *The Cloister and the Hearth*, perhaps Alan Breck in *Kidnapped* if he can manage the dialect, and later Lorna Doone, Jane Eyre, Maggie Tulliver.

Literature is a looking-glass in which we see good and evil: the worthiness of the one, and the destructiveness of the other; and we see these portrayed in lives that we can imagine, understand and feel deeply for, according to the wealth of our experience and the richness of our maturity. And we feel they are portrayed in our lives, for the life we see in the story is like ours, though it is more intense and dramatic. So we can see with striking force what great evil may result from a man's cruel and greedy intent, and what fine action can flower in the face of trouble, and how steadfast courage can persist without hope—glimpses of life lived at its best: so our admiration is stirred, our thoughts and feelings elevated, and our conceptions of what is good and true are renewed and inspired. Thus through the best in literature young people are helped to build up standards of what is right, fitting, and to be fought for in life.

The Problem of Pupils leaving School without having read any Literature. Nearly all countries in the world include in their educational programme the teaching of foreign languages; and one of the main reasons given by all of them is that languages must be learnt so that their literature can be read. But if this is so important, and we must agree that it is, what are we to do about those pupils who leave school without having read any great literature in the foreign language they have learnt, or without having had any read to them ? Very large numbers of pupils in every country do not have a secondary school education that enables them to read the great literature of a foreign country easily enough to profit by it. But educationists do not appear to be perturbed by this fact. They should be. They should ask themselves, and so should we: " Are all these pupils to miss this special help and guidance that is given by great literature ? Are they never to have any introduction to the wealth and wisdom of the greatest of the world's writers, with their vivid and revealing portrayal of character, their manifold and deep concern with human nature, and their rich and exciting stories of man's struggle against indifferent, hostile or destructive forces, and their triumphant revelation of " Man's unconquerable mind " ?

If these pupils have not mastered the foreign language sufficiently for them to read this literature, or to understand enough of it when it is read to them, then nothing more can profitably be said—except the urgent comment that the teaching of the foreign language therefore needs to be intensified and made more competent. But those who have taught boys and girls in Africa, Asia or elsewhere know that pupils at the top of Senior, Middle and Secondary Modern Schools in many parts of the world can profit by having *some* acquaintance with the greatest books of literature, and if not in English, why not in translation ?

But if some of the pupils we have referred to could read some literature, such as *The Rime of the Ancient Mariner*, *Pilgrim's Progress*, *Robinson Crusoe*, *Gulliver's Travels*, *Wuthering Heights*, *The Vicar of Wakefield*, and do not, then there is something wrong. If they do not read some of these, or parts of them, or have some read to them, is it not true that the educational programme of the schools needs drastic scrutiny, and perhaps an overhaul of the syllabus of the top forms ? But something can be done without official action or instruction, and without much trouble. First we ought to feel that the following is conclusive and unanswer-able: that every pupil at the top of a school should not leave without having had some acquaintance with one or two books of great literature, and without knowing that there is a fine storehouse of literary treasures that are his by right if he can read them.

What to do for pupils who cannot read well enough. To begin with, we have to face the fact that a lot cannot be done for pupils whose language learning has not been successful, and they cannot receive much that great literature can give to an intelligent reader. But what can be done, should be done, for one can never tell when and where good seeds may fall and bear good fruit. The least that every teacher could do is to read to his class, and this might do a good deal for some of the pupils. He could read some of the passages that he himself felt were important to him, or had been valuable to him when he was younger. Then, even if many of the pupils did not understand it properly or if some understood only part of it, they might catch some of its good qualities, or some of the excitement or depth of feeling in it, and would without reasoning or exact understanding be aware of its value, just as any appreciative but untrained person becomes aware of the grandeur of some music he does not properly understand. This is one of the simplest and commonest ways of forming a sense of values; and as these pupils are capable of a fine sense of values, they would very likely have achieved something important. They would know too that the book was worth an effort to read, and was one that they might turn to after leaving school. After all, generations of Englishman and women formerly never read any literature; but they heard the Bible read in church and sometimes at home.

At the end of each week or in the last week of the term, a teacher might arrange for special readings to be given to the top classes. These might be given by the head teacher or by an invited visitor or someone of importance locally. During the term, whenever one of the staff falls ill, it is an easy and very welcome plan for one of the others to take a double class and read short stories or a long extract from some interesting book; and if some of the pupils have to sit on the floor, that adds to the occasion for many children. Thus other books can be introduced to the pupils, who if without a teacher would most likely waste time and perhaps cause disturbance.

Then senior pupils can sometimes be encouraged to read one or two of the easier and shorter classics, for much can be done by personal persuasion, and they might be led on in this way to read other books. This is where a well-run school library would be a great asset for promoting wide reading. It has been observed that many pupils at the top of a Middle or Senior School are capable of understanding great literature, though they may not understand every word—do we ourselves understand and read every word ? So that, if these pupils can be helped in the library to make sensible choices of books, the love of reading might be engendered, and a boy's desire for knowledge not go totally unsatisfied.

At first these pupils usually need help to persevere and to get into a story; the teacher's questions often are sufficient for this purpose, for they can help them to remember what has happened in the story in a previous reading, and may stir up some curiosity in what might happen next. These questions are not intended to see if the pupils have understood, but for the far more useful purpose of helping them to see more in the story than they could have imagined by merely listening or by reading silently. They are to help the readers to build up in imagination a full background to make the characters understandable and convincing, and their motives and actions reasonable and natural. In other words, the questions are to train these unobservant and unaccustomed minds to be awake and ready to receive the suggestions and the nourishing influence of good literature. This kind of training is especially necessary, of course, in countries where reading is not a customary habit in the home, and where the resources of great literature are not readily available for those who can enjoy them.

One thing is particularly important at first: the selection of books for these pupils to read, for they may easily be put off by being given dull or difficult texts. But though great literature has been repeatedly referred to, there are not many books and poems in this category that are really suitable for children, especially children of other races and cultures. Nevertheless, there are a number of story-books and poems that may be classed as literature of lesser quality which can act for immature and inexperienced youth in the same way, and with the same values, as great literature acts for mature and critical minds. The adventure stories of our early reading, when read with absorbed attention and growing excitement, with imagination afire in its passionate identification with the hero, and in its vivid participation in his difficulties and dangers, and in his noblest sentiments, too, even if these may be conventional: these are the stories that will inspire young people with hope and desire for noble deeds, and will stimulate their sympathies to form high ideals, and may perhaps sometimes kindle their determination to follow a life of service to the community. These are the stories that will be of value in the education and upbringing of boys and girls; and then when they have learnt to enjoy these stories, they may look for and read the greater works of literature.

Finally in selecting stories for a class to read, there is a further point to remember: literature widens experience. This may well be the strongest reason for planning an ambitious programme of reading for pupils who live in the bush, in distant savannah lands far from any town, who never see the sea or majestic mountains. And children in towns, too, often have far more limited experience than we realize. The disadvantage of this is that children who have limited experience often have limited ideas (unless they are gifted with an abundance of intellectual energy), and their thinking and interests then must necessarily be very limited in number, depth and variety. But wide experience alone can act as a stimulus to the growth and activity of the mental abilities of growing children, and can awaken the sleepy mind to be aware of and to grasp new ideas and new ways of thinking. And the experiences that books can give to a reader can be as powerful an influence on young minds as real experience in everyday life. Even books of no great value to an adult may provide for the mentally starved pupil the first step towards a better understanding of the life around him and towards a simple appreciation of value. Therefore the books of Henty, Marryat, Charles Reade, Orczy, Kipling, Buchan, Melville, Kearton, Tomlinson, Ernest Seton Thompson, and others at this level, might well be considered for this purpose —the widening of experience, and for the purpose of helping pupils to acquire the habit of reading.

Chapter 24

THE MOTHER TONGUE AND FOREIGN LANGUAGE TEACHING

The teaching of the mother tongue in Africa, Asia, and in many other parts of the world to-day, is not always thought to be as necessary and valuable in developing children's minds as it is by educationists in the United Kingdom, Canada, the United States, in other English-speaking countries, and in nearly all countries in Europe. Consequently it has not been given the attention that should be accorded to it. It is evident that the teaching of the vernaculars, in Africa especially, but also widely elsewhere, is rarely considered of very great importance; therefore there has been little improvement in the teaching of the mother tongue compared with the great advances in soundness and thoroughness of method that have been made in the United Kingdom, and in France, Belgium, Switzerland—to pick out a few examples of the countries in Europe that have given special thought and experiment in this field.

It is true that very many teachers from Africa and Asia have studied the new developments in the teaching of the mother tongue in the United States and the United Kingdom; but a majority of these teachers have gone back to their own countries without any conception, or only a poor one, of what is being done by the best teachers in Europe and America. This is partly because it is difficult to perceive exactly what values a teacher is working for, what are his aims, and what special techniques and procedures he is handling in conditions quite new, and often not perceptible, to a visitor from another continent. So, even if such a visitor spends some time in an English, Welsh or American school, he may not learn the secret of the best ways of teaching the mother tongue, especially as the secret lies not solely in method, but in a skilful and intelligent handling of method. Pupils' needs, experience and their upbringing are so different that it is surprising that visitors gain anything at all from what they observe. Especially as the difference between a well handled and an unskilfully handled method is frequently so slight, that an onlooker must miss those finer points in the teaching that give the true value to the training that the pupils are receiving. Then, when the visitor returns to his own country, he is faced with the problem of applying and adapting what he has seen and approved in his studies in European or American schools to his own school, to quite different conditions, and sometimes in another language. Too little thought has been given to this difficult problem. There is also the fact that visitors from other continents are often given too much and too wide a sweep of experience to assimilate, and they want to see too much, instead of making a thorough study of the simple fundamentals.

But this is not the place to point out what could be done to improve the teaching of the mother tongue in various parts of the world. Nevertheless, something must be said on the subject, because the teaching of the mother tongue and the teaching of a foreign language can support and assist each other. For we are dealing here with the teaching of *language*; and whether the language is the mother tongue or a foreign language, some of the methods used in the teaching will be very similar, and most of the principles underlying those methods will be the same. Therefore we may be sure that if the mother tongue is well taught, that teaching will help the learning of a new language; and if a foreign language is taught on sound lines, the training that it gives the pupils will promote a better understanding and a better use of the mother tongue.

There are three main reasons why improvement in the teaching of the mother tongue is highly desirable. First, improvement in handling language is directly favourable to improvement in all kinds of thinking, such as reasoning and other mental operations that make use of words. Second, nearly all children need instruction and specially devised practice in the use of their mother tongue in order to acquire the ability to express themselves with clarity, ease and correctness. The third reason is that those children who acquire some skill in using their mother tongue, have had a good preparation for acquiring similar skills in using a foreign language.

In discussing this subject, and whenever we think about it, we ought to remind ourselves always that all languages— French, German, English, Swahili, Hausa, Hindi, etc.—are used for exactly the same purposes, whether they are used as a mother tongue, as a second and bilingual, or as a strange foreign language. They are used, for instance, for communication, for expressing anything that we have attended to, for recording information, for thinking, for getting what we want, and so on. We have to remember, too, that when we are using a foreign language, we are bringing into play the same linguistic skills as those we use when we speak or write in our mother tongue. Thus, skill in constructing sentences will be active whether we are practising our mother tongue or writing a paragraph in a foreign language; and the skill of understanding meaning from context in a new language will be the same skill that we use when we understand meaning from context in our mother tongue.

We can go further: if a pupil has been taught to use his mother tongue with grammatical correctness, he will be ready to learn to use the new language correctly, for he will be a potential correct-language-user ! He will have acquired habits of attending to correctness of language. So, too, if he has been taught to express his thoughts clearly in his mother tongue, we shall know that he can be taught to express them clearly in the new language; for his mind having achieved clarity of thought and expression will be able to apply that in another language, though he may need special instruction to effect the transfer. Similarly if a speaker talks freely and fluently in his own language, he can soon learn to speak well and easily in another language, when he has mastered its forms and structures. This, however, is not to say that he will not need much training and practice; but it does mean that he will learn quickly if the instruction and training are intelligent and sound. It follows therefore that if we can improve the teaching of both mother tongue and foreign language, our pupils will more quickly master the fundamental skills that are needed for the efficient handling of both languages. It hardly needs emphasizing that in learning a foreign language most pupils need all the help that it is possible to give them if they are to make good use of the new instrument of thought and communication.

It is clear, too, that many of the methods of teaching the mother tongue can be used also in teaching a new language, and vice versa. If a child has learnt to form letters in writing his mother tongue, he will be able to form the letters of the new language, unless the script is different. Then, later, if a pupil learns to punctuate his mother tongue, and has thus learnt the habit of putting in stops, even if not always correctly, he will find it easy to learn to punctuate when he is learning French or English. So, many of the successful methods that a teacher has used in lessons with the mother tongue, should be tried out in teaching the new language. Often some adaptations may have to be made; and usually pupils should be shown carefully how to apply what they learnt in their mother tongue in their learning of another language; for we must never *assume* that habits and skills will be carried over from mother-tongue learning to foreign language learning: they will often be carried over by intelligent pupils, but we must not assume that they will be. So the application and adaptation to the new language has to be demonstrated and illustrated fully, particularly to slow learners.

Let us take another important skill: learning to read. Children who have been taught to read their mother tongue well, can quickly learn to read English after one or two years of oral English. Therefore it will be a great help to pupils who have to learn a foreign language, if the initial teaching of reading the mother tongue in a school is improved and intensified. This particularly applies where a foreign language is the medium of instruction in schools. Similarly, later, if pupils have acquired speed and accuracy in silent reading, they will soon learn to read the new language silently with speed and accuracy. This will affect their whole education favourably, for they will not have to spend burdensome hours and days, and even perhaps weeks, struggling through books (and not taking everything in); because their silent reading is too inefficient. Then they will be able to go ahead in all the subjects that are being studied with the help of books. If we train them to master the same skills in their mother tongue that they need in learning the foreign language, their progress must inevitably increase steadily, and perhaps it will increase rapidly.

For the same reason pupils should be taught to make

competent use of their mother tongue: to explain things clearly and briefly, to report concisely on events, to tell a story, to speak with ease and point, to write strictly to a subject, to make a precise summary of a page or chapter of an informative book. It is essential for them to acquire the skills involved in doing these tasks if they are going on to higher education; and even if they are not, the acquisition of them will increase their intellectual maturity, and make them more capable of thinking, deciding, planning, advising, voting, etc. And these same skills can be useful in learning the new language, and the pupils will be able to write detailed descriptions in the new language, to explain precisely how to do something, how to make something, how to go somewhere. The full use of detail in description and explanation would be learnt first in the mother tongue, and then applied in the new language. Thus the pupils become adept in doing precise and useful work. For the handling of exact detail can be learnt whatever language is being used, and it is essential to master this skill if progress is to continue, and if it is to continue, the harder the tasks should become.

STAGE ONE QUESTIONING

THIS is an example of part of an actual lesson in which the teacher was questioning a class on a passage that had been read silently. The purpose of the questions was to train the pupils to note exactly what the writer had said. The first paragraph to be read was as follows:—" There are six different plants in this picture. If you look at them carefully you will be able to tell what their names are. The first one is a gourd. The gourd is a creeping and climbing plant which is very common in Africa and India. Its fruit is very useful and many people allow the plant to climb over the flat roofs of small huts as they cultivate it in their gardens."

Teacher: " How many kinds of plants are there in the picture ? "

A Pupil: " Six plants."

T.: " Are they all the same ? "

P.: " No."

T.: " Where can you see the plants now ? "

P.: " I can see them in the picture."

T.: " How can you tell what their names are ? "

P.: " By looking at them carefully."

T.: " What is the name of the plant in the first picture ? "

P.: " A gourd."

T.: " What kind of a plant is it ? "

P.: " A creeping and climbing plant."

T.: " In what countries is it very common ? "

P.: " In India and Africa."

T.: " Has it any fruit ? "

P.: " Yes, it has fruit."

T.: " Where does the writer say the plant is allowed to climb ? "

P.: " It is allowed to climb in gardens and huts."

T.: " No, the writer does not say that. Have you ever seen a gourd climbing *inside* a hut ?—Next boy."

P.: " They are allowed to climb over the flat roofs of small huts."

T.: " Good ! Why do people sometimes allow it to climb there ? "

P.: " Because the plant is very useful to them."

T.: " What are the roofs like, that the plant climbs over ? "

P.: " The roofs are flat."

T.: " What are the huts with these roofs like ? "

P.: " The huts are small."

T.: " What does the writer say many people do in their gardens ? "

P.: " Grow gourds."

T.: " Where do many people grow gourds ? "

P.: " In their gardens."

Then followed further silent reading:—" Besides those which are cultivated, there are many climbing plants which grow wild on walls, on fences and in the forest. Those which climb up fences do so by turning themselves round and round a post until they reach the top. Those which grow in the hot wet forests of Africa, India and South America climb up the big trees by turning themselves round the trunks or round the branches. Some of them are very long. Their long thin stalks reach to the tops of the highest trees in order to get into the sunshine above the tree-tops."

T.: " What are wild plants ? "

P.: " Wild plants are plants which grow by themselves."

T.: " Good. But what word does the writer use ? "

P.: " Wild plants are plants which are not cultivated."[1]

T.: " Where does the writer say that wild climbing plants grow ? "

P.: " On fences, on walls and in the forest."

T.: " How do climbing plants climb up fences ? "

P.: " By turning round the fence."

T.: " What parts of the fence ? "

P.: " The posts."

T.: " What are the forests of South America like ? "

P.: " They are wet and hot."

T.: " Where do climbing plants climb in the forest ? "

P.: " Climbing plants grow up the big trees."

T.: " How high do climbing plants climb in the forest ? "

P.: " Climbing plants grow as high as the tall trees."

T.: " Why do they climb so high ? "

P.: " Because it wants to get the sunshine."

T.: " Because *it* . . .? What's this *it* ? Because . . .? "[2]

P.: " Because they want to get the sunshine."

T.: " What is interesting about these climbing plants ? "

P.: " The way in which they grow round and round."

T.: " What do these climbing plants do to get to the top of a post ? "

P.: " They turn round and round it."

T.: " What do they do to get to the end of a branch ? "

P.: " They turn round and round the branch."

(and so on)

---

[1] The word had been learnt previously, otherwise its meaning would have been made more clear, *e.g.* " How do you *cultivate* plants ? "

[2] Mistakes are usually corrected without explanation in a lesson of this kind.

IMPROVEMENTS TO WRITTEN WORK

Examples of Suggestions

1. IMPROVING CLARITY OF THOUGHT AND EXPRESSION

(All examples taken from pupils' actual compositions.)

(i) " The Hyena had just finished sacrificing when the boy knocked at the door. Then when *he* opened the door, he saw . . ."

(*Note*.—It is not quite certain who opened the door; therefore change ' he ' to ' the Hyena ' or ' the boy,' according to who opened the door.)

(ii) " Spider collected all the pestles and hid them. When the people wanted to pound some maize they looked in every corner of the room, but they found none."

(*Note*.—Does the word ' none ' refer to maize or pestles ? It is not certain, though the sense tells us that it was the pestles that were hidden; but it would be clearer if ' for a pestle ' were added after ' the corner of the room.')

(iii) " When they were about to start, Chameleon went to Zebra and held his tail."

(*Note*.—The words ' went to ' are very vague: did Chameleon go up to his side or behind him or to his head ? It is not clear: so change to ' went behind Zebra.' Then if we write ' held his tail ' that might imply ' so that he could not get away '; but if we say ' held *on to* ' that suggests Chameleon was swinging on it or was supported by it.')

(iv) " They worked so hard that when they were going home, the farmer gave them two goats."

(*Note*.—It is not clear when the goats were given. Was it on the way home or just as they were starting ? Therefore change to: ' before they went home '; or ' just before they went home,' which would be still clearer.)

2.   GETTING RID OF VAGUENESS OF VOCABULRRY

(i) " Mr. Monkey got some soap and rubbed it on a rock in the middle of the path so that Mr. Spider might come and fall."

(*Note*.—The words ' come and fall ' are vague. So change to ' might come along and slip down ' or ' so that when Spider walked on it he would fall down.' The words ' slip ' or ' slip down ' are more exact than ' fall,' and ' fall down ' suggests he would fall down on the ground and so hurt himself.)

(ii) " He took his father's things and wore them."

(*Note*.—Actually he took only clothes, not other things, so ' clothes ' would be more exact than ' things.' The words ' wore them ' tells us he had them on for some time; but in the story he had them on only a very short time: what did he really do: ' He *put them on* '—that tells us exactly what he did with them.)

(iii) " In the dark forest Spider took hold of a foolish deer."

(*Note*.—The word ' took ' does not tell us whether the action was sudden in case the deer might spring away, or gentle in order not to frighten the deer. So alter to ' seized ' or ' caught hold of ' or ' gently caught hold of '—according to what he actually did.)

3. IMPROVING CLARITY BY ADDING DETAILS

(i) " They both fell asleep. At that moment a hungry hyena was passing by, and was so happy that he went and told his family to ... quet."

... happy ? No reason is given, ... both asleep ' or ' and saw ... a feast.')

... the hunter. But the hunter ...

... d in the story that the hunter knew magic. So change to ... d so turned himself . . .')

... ll the hunter; they tried to ... which the old hunter was ...

... climbing the tree ? Was it ... ? Earlier we are told that ... e-wood; so add ' the old ... o get fire-wood, so they all ...

... fall, a small frog under the ... fall, but to stand upright."

... did the frog not want the ... ause it did not want to be ...

... y continues: " The hunter then called his

Cassettes
ILFORD 35 mm MINIATURE FILMS

Loading and unloading

To load this cassette in the camera, attach the f... film (protruding from the cassette) to the camera... and insert the cassette in the cassette chamber; w... light and take care not to pull out more film tha... for attachment. Then, close the camera back and... film according to the instructions issued with the... the full length is exposed, rewind the film int... before opening the camera back.

Outdoor exposure guide

Set lens aperture as indicated in table and set shutter speed to :
1/25 sec for Pan
1/50 sec for FP3
1/100 sec for HP3
1/200 sec for HPS

Type of subject	Sunshine, blue sky	Slightly overcast sky	Dull
Landscapes. Seascapes. Beach scenes. Snow scenes.	f/22	f/16	f/11
Buildings. Gardens. Distant figures or groups.	f/16	f/11	f/8
Close-ups of people or groups.	f/11	f/8	f/5.6
English			

Ilford Limited Ilford Ess...
L 65

famous dog. And so the dog came and saw all the animals round the tree."

(*Note.*—We are not told that the tree obeyed the frog, so add ' and so it stood upright.' Is the man still up the tree ? It might be better to add ' But as the man could not get down because the animals were all waiting at the bottom of it to catch him, he called his famous dog.')

Appendix C

THE USEFULNESS OF MISTAKES

It will be recognized by all teachers of languages who work as craftsmen that pupils' mistakes are not only inevitable but can actually be useful. The reasons for this are that mistakes reveal the difficulties that are being faced by the pupils; they indicate where drill exercises have been inadequate, and they bring to light failures in hearing and recognition. On the other hand, if mistakes are occurring very rarely, the teacher may suspect that his pupils are being practised within too narrow limits of vocabulary and structure, and are not practising the use of the language they have already learnt in a sufficiently wide range of subject, situation or experience—they are being under-taught.

The up-to-date teacher, therefore, does not become anxious and disturbed in mind when mistakes appear with some frequency. He does, however, take action: he makes a collection of common errors, and then attempts to diagnose their causes. This simple form of investigation may lead to the discovery that certain types of common error are caused by pupils using wrong words, grammatical forms and structures on the pattern of their mother tongue. To make such mistakes is a perfectly natural linguistic habit, as the force of analogy is an extremely strong influence on language habits. It is particularly strong because the mother tongue all over the world is learnt mainly by imitation, for analogy is an imitative process, fostered by a natural desire for repetitions and similarities, rather than by the more creative and individual delight in variety, change and contrast.

When some of the causes of common errors have been diagnosed, special measures may then be devised to prevent or combat the making of these common mistakes. But, unfortunately, the devising of these special measures affords unusual opportunities for unsound treatment, for instance, such as putting emphasis on errors by directing undue attention to them and repeating them, thus favouring their recurrence; or isolating them from their contexts, thus making them largely meaningless, and leaving them outside the main stream of language that the pupils are using. In addition, these special measures will be useless if they present mere lists of examples in the mother tongue with the correct forms in the foreign language in a parallel list opposite.

Corrective exercises have to provide (*a*) something for the pupils to say or write, that is, some more positive occupation than listening; (*b*) sentences or short paragraphs to be imitated, completed or added to; (*c*) if possible no opportunities in these sentences and paragraphs for mistakes other than the common mistake that is receiving attention, *e.g.* as in Sentence Completion Exercises and Substitution Tables; (*d*) a series of exercises directed at each common error; (*e*) as full a context as possible for each sentence, *e.g.* as in Complex Sentences requiring the completion or addition of one or two single words, or as in a sequence of sentences on one subject, such as (1) I was waiting for the . . .; (2) My brother was waiting for . . . too; (3) When we saw . . .; (4) We saw that this . . .was not the usual . . . ; (5) The . . . that came every morning was green; (6) This . . . was red.

In diagnosing the causes of common errors, the following should not be overlooked: (*a*) too little written work; (*b*) insufficient repetitions in exercises of new items of language, especially Tenses; (*c*) too little correcting of written work by pupils, or this being done carelessly; (*d*) too little application of the grammar that is explained by the teacher; (*e*) pupils' poor eyesight or hearing; (*f*) too frequent copying of mistakes from books within eye-range (a more prevalent cause than many teachers realize).

Bibliography (Selected)

Part I—The Teaching of English as a Foreign Language

(Pronunciation and Articulation)

Author	Title	Publisher	Date
ALLEN, W. S.	*Living English Speech*	Longmans Green	1954
ARMSTRONG, L. E. and WARD, I. C.	*A Handbook of English Intonation*	Heffer	1949
CLARK, A. M.	*Spoken English*	Oliver & Boyd	1947
JONES, D.	*An English Pronouncing Dictionary* (9th ed.)	Dent	1948
SHILLAN, D.	*Spoken English*	Longmans Green	1954

Author	Title	Publisher	Date
ALLEN, W. S.	*Living English Structure*	Longmans Green	1950
BALL, W. J.	*Conversational English*	Longmans Green	1953
BLACK, N. F.	*English for the Non-English*	Regina Book Shop Ltd., Regina, Canada	1952
CAMPION, H.	*Lectures on Teaching English in India.*	Oxford Univ. Press	1933
COALE, W. B. and SMITH, M. E.	*Successful Practices in Teaching English to Bilingual Children in Hawaii.*	Bulletin No. 14. Office of Education, Washington, D.C.	1937
COLEMAN, A. (ed.)	*English Teaching in the South-West.*	The American Council of Education	1940
ELLIOTT, A. V. P. and GURREY, P.	*Language Teaching in African Schools.*	Longmans Green	1940
FAUCETT, L.	*The Teaching of English in the Far East.*	Harrap	1927
FRENCH, F. C.	*The Teaching of English Abroad.* Vols. I, II, III.	Oxford Univ. Press	1948
FRIES, C. C.	*Teaching and Learning English as a Foreign Language.*	Ann Arbor. Univ. of Michigan Press	1945
GATENBY, E. V.	*English as a Foreign Language.*	Longmans Green	1944
GURREY, P.	*The Teaching of English in Africa, Asia, the Mediterranean and Elsewhere.*	Unesco, Paris (mimeo.)	1952
HOARD, LUCY C.	*Teaching English to the Spanish-speaking Child in Primary Grades.*	El Paso, New Texas, U.S.A.	

Author	Title	Publisher	Date
ISIDRO, Y. *and* SANTES, A.	*Development of Written English Expression of Filipino Children.*	Univ. of Chicago Press	1937
LEAVITT, L. W.	*The Teaching of English to Foreign Students.*	Longmans Green	1940
MENDILOW, A. A. *and* MORRIS, I.	*A Concise Guide to the Teaching of English to Foreigners.*	Central Press, Jerusalem	1940
MORRIS, I.	*The Teaching of English as a Second Language.*	Macmillan	1945
	The Art of Teaching English as a Living Language	Macmillan	1954
PALMER, H. E.	*The Teaching of Oral English.*	Longmans Green	1940
PATTISON, B.	*English Teaching in the World Today* (Studies in Education)	Evans	1950
POWERS, F. F. *and* HETZLER, M.	*Successful Methods of Teaching English to Bilingual Children in Seattle.*	Bulletin No. 76. Dept. of Interior, Washington	1938
RYBURN, W. M.	*Suggestions for the Teaching of English in India.*	Oxford Univ. Press	1933
STOREY, H. R.	*Lessons in English for Native Schools.*	Lovedale Press, Cape Town	—
THOMPSON, M. S. H. *and* WYATT, H. G.	*The Teaching of English in India.* (3rd ed.)	Oxford Univ. Press	1935
WEST, M.	*A General Service List of English Words*	Longmans Green	1953
	Learning to Read a Foreign Language	Longmans Green	1955
	Language in Education.	Longmans Green	1929
	On Learning to Speak a Foreign Language.	Longmans Green	1933
WILLIAMS, H.	*English as the Second Language.*	Oxford Univ. Press	1936
WOHLFARTH *and* BERMEJO	*Methods of Teaching English in First and Second Grades.*	Philippine Book Co.	1928
WREN, P. C.	*The Direct Method of Teaching English in Indian Schools.*	Longmans Green	1927
THE BRITISH COUNCIL	*English Language Teaching.* Periodical.	65 Davies Street, London, W.1	—

PART II—TEACHING FOREIGN LANGUAGES

AGARD, F. B. *and* DUNKEL, H. B.	*An Investigation of Second Language Teaching*	Ginn	1948
ASSCN. OF ASSISTANT MASTERS IN SECONDARY SCHOOLS	*The Teaching of Modern Languages*	Univ. of London Press	1949

Author	Title	Publisher	Date
ˈKINS, H. G. and HUTTON, H. L.	The Teaching of Modern Foreign Languages in School and University.	Arnold	1920
ˌKER, F. M.	The Teaching of French.	Houghton Mifflin, Boston	1931
ˌTEMAN, G. C.	Aids to Modern Language Teaching.	Constable	1925
ːACH, T.	Modern Language Teaching and Learning with Gramophone and Radio.	Heffer	1930
ˌLL, C. Y.	Teaching Modern Languages to Adults.	Harrap	1947
ˈNZIES, D.	Learning Our Language.	Longmans Green	1940
ˈNGERS, H.	The History and Principles of Vocabulary Control.	Woerden, Holland	1947
ˈNGERS, H. and DE LA COURT, A.	The Rational Teaching of Languages.	Wolters, Groningen	1935
ˌERETON, C.	Modern Language Teaching.	Univ. of London Press	1930
ˈCHANAN, M. A. and McPHEE, C. D.	An Annotated Bibliography of Modern Language Methodology.	Univ. of Toronto Press	1938
ˌOSSET, Fr.	L'enseignement des langues vivantes et la comprehension internationale.	Unesco, Paris (mimeo)	—
	Didactique des Langues Vivantes.	Didier, Bruxelles	1949
ˈLE, R. D.	Modern Foreign Languages and Their Teaching. (Revised 1937 by Tharp, J. B.)	Appleton, New York	1931
ˈLEMAN, A.	Experiments and Studies in Modern Language Teaching.	Univ. of Chicago Press	1934
ˌAWFORD, C. C. and LEITZELL, E. M.	Learning New Languages.	Los Angeles	1930
ˈMMINGS, T. L. P.	How to Learn a Language.	Kegan Paul	1916
ˌNKEL, H. B.	Second Language Learning	Ginn	1948
ˈE, R. H.	A Summary of Reports on the Modern Foreign Languages.	Macmillan, New York	1929
ˈE, R. H. (ed.)	An Analytical Bibliography of Modern Language Teaching. 1937-42.	Columbia Univ. Press	1942
ˈNDLAY, J. J.	Modern Language Learning.	Gregg Pub. Co.	1929
ˈNSHENA, K. A.	Methodology in Foreign Language Teaching.	Moscow	1930
ˈLLETTE, C. C. and KEATING, L. C. and VIENS, P. L.	Teaching a Modern Language.	Crofts & Co., New York	1942

Author	Title	Publisher	Date
HAGBOLDT, P.	*Language Learning.*	Univ. of Chicago Press	193
HANDSCHIN, C. H.	*Methods of Teaching Modern Languages.*	World Book Co., New York	192
	Modern Language Teaching.	World Book Co., New York	194
HEDGCOCK, F. A.	*Practical French Teaching.*	Pitman	193
HENMON, V. A. C.	*Achievement Tests in Modern Foreign Languages.*	New York	192
HUSE, H. R.	*The Psychology of Foreign Language Study.*	N. Carolina Univ. Press	193
JESPERSEN, O.	*How to Teach a Foreign Language.*	Allen & Unwin	190
KIRKMAN, F. B.	*The Teaching of Foreign Languages.*	Univ. Tutorial Press	190
KITTSON, E. C.	*Theory and Practice of Language Teaching.*	Clarendon Press Oxford Univ. Press	192
O'SHEA, M. V.	*The Reading of Modern Foreign Languages.*	Bulletin No. 16. Washington, D.C.	192
PALMER, H. E.	*The Scientific Study and Teaching of Languages.*	Harrap	191
	The Principles of Language Study.	Harrap	192
	The Oral Method of Teaching Languages.	Heffer	192
PALMER, H. E. and REDMAN, H. V.	*This Language Learning Business.*	Harrap	193
STOTT, D. H.	*Language Teaching in the New Education.*	Univ. of London Press	194
SWEET, H.	*The Practical Study of Languages.*	Dent	189
WOOD, B. D.	*New York Experiments with New Type Modern Language Tests.*	Macmillan	-
WINTER, A. J. S.	*The African Primary School.*	Lutterworth Press	-

PART III—OFFICIAL PUBLICATIONS

MINISTRY OF EDUCATION, ENGLAND. *The Teaching and Organization of Mode Languages.* H.M.S.O., London. 1912.

MINISTRY OF EDUCATION, ENGLAND. *The Position of French in grant-aid Secondary Schools in England.* H.M.S.O., London. 1926.

MINISTRY OF EDUCATION, ENGLAND. *The Position of German in grant-aid Secondary Schools in England.* H.M.S.O., London. 1929.

MINISTRY OF EDUCATION, ENGLAND. *The Teaching of Foreign Languages in Mode Schools.* H.M.S.O., London. 1930.

MINISTRY OF EDUCATION, ENGLAND. *The Future of Secondary Education in Wales.* H.M.S.O., London. 1949.

MINISTRY OF EDUCATION (WELSH DEPARTMENT), ENGLAND. *Language Teaching in Primary Schools.* H.M.S.O., London. 1945.

SCOTTISH EDUCATION DEPARTMENT. *Modern Languages in Secondary Schools.* H.M.S.O., London or Edinburgh. 1951.

MINISTRY OF EDUCATION, FRANCE. *Instructions générales pour l'enseignement des langues vivantes.* Paris. 1951.

MINISTRY OF EDUCATION, SWITZERLAND. *L'enseignement des langues vivantes.* Conférence Internationale de l'Instruction Publique. Geneva. 1937.

DEPARTMENT OF PUBLIC EDUCATION, SOUTH AFRICA. *The Primary School.* Cape Times Ltd., Cape Town. 1928.

DEPARTMENT OF PUBLIC EDUCATION, SOUTH AFRICA. *The Primary School Course for Native Schools.* Caxton Printing Works. Cape Town. 1929.

MINISTRY OF EDUCATION, EGYPT. *The Teaching of English in Egyptian Girls' Schools.* By Miss M. E. Carter. Government Press. Cairo. 1936.

MINISTRY OF EDUCATION, THE GOLD COAST. *Report on Research into the Teaching and Learning of English in the Gold Coast.* By P. Gurrey. Government Printer. Accra. 1953.

AMERICAN AND CANADIAN COMMITTEE ON MODERN LANGUAGES. *Studies in Modern Languages.* Vol. XVII. The Macmillan Co. New York. 1930.

DEPARTMENT OF EDUCATION, CALIFORNIA. *Guide for Teachers of Non-English-Speaking Children.* Sacramento. 1932.

AMERICAN COUNCIL ON EDUCATION. Minutes of a Conference on *The Teaching of English as a Foreign Language.* Columbia University. Dec., 1937.

U.N.E.S.C.O. *African Languages and English in Education.* Paris. 16e Avenue Kléber No. 19. June, 1953.

ASSOCIATION OF BRITISH SCHOOLMASTERS IN EGYPTIAN GOVERNMENT SCHOOLS. *Report on the Teaching of English in the Government Secondary Schools and Intermediate Schools of Commerce.* Cairo. 1933.

INDEX